STOLEN CHILD

Praise for *Stolen Child*

This book is an outstretched hand. A gift to anyone who has sought to understand the mysterious nature of OCD and its isolating, bewildering consequences. This is a tale of tenderness and devotion, a portrait of the importance of community, and a story of surprising, unexpected light.

— Alison Wearing, author of *Confessions of a Fairy's Daughter* and *Honeymoon in Purdah*

Gough's straight ahead style is seductive. She draws you in. You stay in.

— Brian Doyle, author of *Angel Square* and *Up to Low*

What do you do when your child is stricken with a disorder whose cure is not at all certain? If you are a rational skeptic like Laurie Gough you research everything ever written on the disorder and apply the methods of science and reason to solve the problem, without resorting to superstition or the supernatural. *Stolen Child* is beautifully written and emotionally evocative, but it is not just about OCD. It is about the power of reason ... and love ... to overcome adversity, a book that belongs among the classics of parenting.

— Michael Shermer, author of *Why People Believe Weird Things*, *The Believing Brain*, and *The Moral Arc*

People use the term "OCD" casually, often with a snicker. But *Stolen Child* demonstrates beautifully the devastation that the disease can bring, and the love that a family brings to fight it. It's a heartfelt story of a family transformed by OCD, told with compassion and honesty.

— Jim Davies, cognitive scientist and author of *Riveted*

STOLEN CHILD

A Mother's Journey to Rescue Her Son
from Obsessive Compulsive Disorder

LAURIE GOUGH

DUNDURN
TORONTO

Interior and cover design: Laura Boyle
Printer: Webcom
Excerpt on page 154 from *Once a Witch* by Carolyn MacCollough. Copyright © 2009 by Carolyn MacCullough. Reprinted by permission of Houghton Mifflin Harcourt Publishing Company.

Library and Archives Canada Cataloguing in Publication

Gough, Laurie, 1964-, author
     Stolen child : a mother's journey to rescue her son from obsessive compulsive disorder / Laurie Gough.

Issued in print and electronic formats.

ISBN 978-1-4597-3591-0 (paperback).--ISBN 978-1-4597-3592-7 (pdf).--ISBN 978-1-4597-3593-4 (epub)

1. Obsessive-compulsive disorder in children. 2. Obsessive-compulsive disorder--Patients--Biography. 3. Obsessive-compulsive disorder--Treatment. 4. Gough, Laurie, 1964- --Family. 5. Mothers and sons. I. Title.

RJ506.O25G68 2016   618.92'852270092   C2016-903443-7
                                                                                          C2016-903444-5

1   2   3   4   5   20   19   18   17   16

We acknowledge the support of the **Canada Council for the Arts** and the **Ontario Arts Council** for our publishing program. We also acknowledge the financial support of the **Government of Canada** through the **Canada Book Fund** and **Livres Canada Books**, and the **Government of Ontario** through the **Ontario Book Publishing Tax Credit** and the **Ontario Media Development Corporation**.

VISIT US AT
Dundurn.com | @dundurnpress | Facebook.com/dundurnpress | Pinterest.com/dundurnpress

Dundurn
3 Church Street, Suite 500
Toronto, Ontario, Canada
M5E 1M2

Come away, O human child!
To the waters and the wild
With a faery, hand in hand.
For the world's more full of weeping than you can understand.

— William Butler Yeats, "The Stolen Child"

To Rob and Quinn

AUTHOR'S NOTE

OCD can be a cruel illness. But it is also treatable. My son has been brave enough to let me tell this story openly, understanding that you wouldn't shy away from telling people you had diabetes so why shy away from telling people you have or once had OCD? He also understands that this book might inspire and motivate others whose lives have been touched by OCD and give them the strength to fight for the lives they deserve.

A ten-year-old auburn-haired boy gazes out at the choppy slate-blue waters of Lake Ontario. Down the shore he sees men repairing an old red ship in need of paint, a ship that doesn't fit with the gleaming white sailboats and yachts in the harbour. Behind him, people amble along the boardwalk, some holding hands but mostly they're too hot for holding hands. Some are lying flat on the grass where it's cooler. Even though the sun is now slanted low in the sky, everyone is still heat-struck and limp from the day's sweltering temperatures. Gulls squawk just above the boy's head, and across the water he sees the chlorophyll green of the Toronto Islands. Suddenly, without warning, he flings a fistful of ashes toward the sky. He watches the ashes as they catch the wind, swirl into a cloud above his head and float out like a silent just-remembered song over the lake. At their highest point in the air, the boy shouts something. He shouts two words that the people on the grass and the people walking by that evening overhear, something that makes them wonder if the boy is all right.

He shouts, "Fuck off!"

It's now 1936 and another ten-year-old auburn-haired boy is also in Toronto, but this boy is walking home from school. The boy is wearing a faded Chicago Cubs baseball cap and is craning his neck to look up into the trees for birds. He suddenly stops walking when a thought occurs to him. It's a dark thought. It has never entered his mind until this moment. It creeps over him slowly, like fog, until he's engulfed in an all-encompassing frozen fear. Anyone watching from a window might think the boy is trying to understand a timeless human riddle. They might wonder if the boy is all right. He's not moving. He's just standing there.

PROLOGUE

People often ask me when I'll write another travel memoir. I usually say I'm too busy trying to make a living as a writer to write another book, or that most of the stories I write end up online anyway. Mainly, the reason I haven't written another book about my travels is that since becoming a mother, I don't travel the way I used to. I haven't taken off for any year-long escapades to wild out-of-the-way places for years. It's too risky with a kid. Now I travel to safer, easier places.

If only.

My recent journey was to a land far more frightening than any I'd ever visited, a land so foreign and strange that I barely knew where to step, always searching for a map where no map had been made, frantically groping for the exit door, the border crossing back to familiar territory. I barely knew this land, had only heard vague rumours of its existence, smatterings of conversations, an off-hand remark about it once in a Bruce Springsteen interview.

Really, it was a land I knew nothing about.

CHAPTER 1

Dear Dr. Jabour,

My husband and I are desperate for help. Our ten-year-old son has developed severe obsessive compulsive disorder. It began mildly in the spring but in the past couple of months it has ramped up alarmingly. He can no longer function at school, or even get to school since he can no longer walk or ride his bike there without getting stuck on the way. He is continually falling into trances where we can't reach him and is obsessed with the notion that his dead grandpa will come back to life. He performs ever-changing rituals that he believes will bring his grandpa back, despite how many times we've told him that nobody returns from the dead. A short time ago, he was a regular, bright, happy-go-lucky kid who climbed trees, rode a unicycle, played soccer, got A's in school, and loved talking about cars. Now he wants to die. This is a child so wracked with anxiety and strange behaviour that we barely recognize him. We want our son back. Can you help us? We live in Quebec but are willing to come to Los Angeles for treatment.

Eight months earlier, Wakefield, Quebec: Quinn and I were walking down the steep hill of our gravel road into the village, snow crunching beneath our feet. It was February, when the bleak lid of winter hides the sun, pale and heartless, behind a flat undistinguished grey. I looked at my son trudging behind me and sighed. "You don't seem very happy these days, Quinn. I know the weather's lousy but where's my happy little boy?"

Sudden tears pooled in his eyes, then spilled down his cheeks. He stopped walking and what he said tore a rip in my chest: "I'm *not* happy. I used to be. But I haven't been happy since Grandpa died."

Six months had passed since my dad had died and still Quinn was crying himself to sleep at night. His sadness usually descended on him when he was tired, after I'd read him a story at night and he was fighting sleep. But lately, he seemed mournful at random times of the day. We tried everything we could think of to comfort him, told him that some kids, like myself and his dad, didn't have grandparents we remembered and that Quinn was lucky to have been so close to his grandpa, that grief is the price you pay for loving someone. I told him that he'd always have the memory of his grandpa, even when he himself was old, that nothing you truly love is ever really lost. I told him that his grandpa lived much longer than anyone thought he would, and that he had led a long, happy life until the end. I told him that maybe, just maybe, he wasn't entirely gone, that maybe he was somehow still around, in a different way, and who was I to say for sure? I would always cringe a little as I said this and didn't say it often. I didn't want to say things I wasn't sure of myself. Saying that kind of thing felt like administering opium to ease his pain. It was easy to see how religions and gods and stories of an afterlife were invented. It seemed to me they must have come about exactly at times like these, to spare our children and ourselves from anguish.

But none of what I said seemed to help much. What Quinn claimed he was most sad about was that he never got to say goodbye. "If only I'd known the last time we visited him that he was going to die in two weeks, I could have told him goodbye." It was such a wrenching thought that he could hardly get the words out, his face crumpling as he cried inconsolably. All I could do was hug him and think back to our week-long visit last July. One night after dinner my dad had been sketching a baseball diamond at the kitchen table and — with this Jimmy Stewart drawl — he'd been teaching Quinn some baseball rules. On another day they'd actually played catch outside beside my mother's rose bushes like they'd done when Quinn was younger, although by then my dad was eighty-six with a wonky heart and had to take things easy. Quinn said later it was like throwing and catching a ball in slow motion. It was also the visit when my dad had mentioned that Quinn's side-swept bangs reminded him a little of Justin Bieber and we all busted out laughing at the revelation that my dad, never adept at recognizing faces or knowing pop culture, not only knew who Justin Bieber was but had taken in the rockstar's hairstyle.

On the morning we left, as we were packing for the seven-hour road trip back to our home in Wakefield, Quebec, my mother had called out from the kitchen, "Where's Quinn?" and I replied that Quinn was out on the lawn playing croquet.

"Quinn's out on the lawn doing cocaine?" said my dad, chuckling from the living room where he was reading the *Globe and Mail.* My dad's hearing was terrible. He was forever mishearing things and quoting them back to us. Quinn always thought this was a riot.

Moments later we were all out in the driveway with the car packed, my husband Rob bungee-cording our bikes and Quinn's unicycle to the bike rack. As I hugged and kissed my dad goodbye, did I imagine that he held me a moment longer than usual? I remember a moment of confusion in my dad's watery-blue eyes, as if he wanted to say something but stopped himself. Did he know something? The thought crossed my mind at the time, as it often did, that this could be the last time I'd see him. In the previous year my dad had become alarmingly thin, a diminished frail twin of the strong, handsome, athletic man I'd known all my life. Of course I knew Quinn wouldn't be thinking of death. Death had never touched him in the nine years of his life. He'd never even had a pet die because we'd never had one. Should I have mentioned something to Quinn that day? Told him to give his grandpa a second hug just in case?

Two weeks later my mother called. We'd been sweating through a heat wave most of the summer and Quinn and I were about to bike down the hill to cannonball into the river off our neighbourhood dock when the phone rang. Her voice sounded small and faraway. "Your dad's had a stroke. He's in the hospital. When he woke up this morning he sat up and asked if he sounded funny. I told him he did." As my mother spoke, my heart began beating so violently I could feel it in my throat. I'd been dreading this call for years, had always wondered how it would go, what the circumstances would be. "So I went to call an ambulance and while I was on the phone in the kitchen I heard a crash. He'd gotten up and fallen. They took him to the hospital. Laurie, they don't think he'll come back. They think he's in a coma."

"I'm coming," I tell her. "I'll be there as soon as I can."

For reasons that would seem strange to me later, instead of all three of us driving down to my hometown of Guelph, Ontario, where my parents lived, I decided I'd take a bus there by myself. I don't know what my line of thinking was. Perhaps I was in denial, thinking my dad would get better and I needn't bother Rob and Quinn with the long drive. Or perhaps I thought this was too private or intimate or sad to share. I felt as if I were free-falling. Seeing my fellow passengers on the bus and all the people out the window carrying on with normal life astounded me. How could they be so happy? How could they be so oblivious to death and despair?

The next four days were a blur of hospital visits, sleepless nights, and trying to console my despondent, heartsick, nerve-wracked mother who hadn't slept for more than a few hours since my father had had his stroke. I never saw my father conscious in those days and never would again, but somehow, holding his papery pale hand in the hospital room and talking to him calmed the rudderless tilt-a-whirl that was rampaging inside me. I was able to say goodbye to my lovely kind dad who had been such a colourful influence on my life. He was a geographer and a lover of maps and any road leading to some place new. In the 1940s when he was in his teens and early twenties, he'd hitchhiked around North America by himself, usually sitting on the outside rumble seat if there was one — better views that way, he always said. Then, in the 1950s, he'd spent years tramping around Europe — when a bottle of wine in Spain was a dime, a meal was a nickel — and canoe-tripping in Northern Ontario. Every summer when I was a kid, my parents would pack up our tent trailer and family car — a rusty Ford Falcon station wagon that they'd had for years — and we'd set off on a camping trip. We'd go to the Maritimes, the Canadian Prairies, New England, the Great Lakes, the Rockies, Quebec, the Appalachians. Every summer was different. My sister, who was older, hated that car and those camping trips — she always wanted to stay at the Holiday Inn — but I didn't. Those camping trips, and my dad, cultivated my love of the open road.

My dad had written a letter years earlier saying that under no circumstances did he want any life support machines keeping him alive if he were beyond the point of reasonable repair, so we honoured his wishes and let him die naturally. By the time I got back home, and Rob and Quinn were picking me up at the bus station in Ottawa, I knew he'd only have a couple more days left since his brain was so damaged. On the car ride home, I turned to face Quinn and tell him his grandpa was gone.

"I know," he said, before his face crumpled into an anguish I'd never seen on him before. I crawled over the seat into the back to hold him and he sobbed the entire half-hour drive home to Wakefield, his small warm body juddering against mine the whole way. He didn't stop crying that night until he was asleep.

The death of his grandpa seemed to plunge Quinn into an existential crisis. His grief was heart-wrenching, intense, and alarming. Other than being shy, like my dad, and sensitive, Quinn had always been a fairly normal kid — I once even lamented jokingly to my friend Tina that Quinn was *too* normal, meaning he didn't have much of a zany artistic bent, although he liked to draw, and could be truly funny in a dry-witted way. Mostly, he loved running and playing soccer; knew the make, model, and year of every vehicle that passed; had gobbled up all the Harry Potter books, and skied with his grade four friends after school at the local ski hill. He had been a regular happy kid. So who was this depressive child weeping into his pillow every night? Was it death itself that terrified him? The stark unimaginable realization that this is all going to end some day for all of us? Was he afraid of his own death? Of ours?

"No," he kept insisting, when I asked. "I'm sad about Grandpa."

Somewhere or somehow we'd missed something in helping Quinn deal with his grandpa's death. Six months after my dad died, I realized that Quinn was doing his grieving all on his own. He was alone in his mourning. My mother was also deeply grief-stricken — she and my dad had been married for fifty-three years — but since she lived a day's drive away, we only saw her every couple of months. As for myself, I'd been weirdly fine. Sometimes I thought that grief would sneak up on me once the shock wore off. But I came to realize that I wasn't in shock. I seemed to have fully accepted my dad's death.

One day, when I had been in my second year at university, my dad, who was a professor there, had cancelled his class and gone to the hospital because he felt sick — he actually took a city bus to the hospital since he didn't drive to work. That night he went into cardiac arrest and my mother had watched in alarm as six men had stormed into the hospital room to jump-start his heart back to life. Apparently, he had a virus around his heart, something the doctors hadn't seen often and something that could happen even to someone in his fifties who was trim and fit like he was. A week later, my mother and I followed behind the ambulance that was taking my dad to Saint Michael's Hospital in Toronto. We were told there was a good chance he wouldn't make it there alive.

I remember feeling as if a blazing fire had suddenly been stomped out inside me, leaving a hollow, chilled shell. One moment my life had consisted of staying up until 3:00 a.m. with my friends at the university's International House — a campus residence full of young eccentric idealists from around the world; dancing to The Clash, Talking Heads, and U2 at the campus bar; protesting the contras who were currently taking over Nicaragua; discussing apartheid and whether or not Nelson Mandela would ever be free; listening to Neil Young, Joni Mitchell, and Bruce Cockburn on country drives in my friend's Chevette; planning the next dance party in the basement of our residence; and attending classes for a degree in International Development. Occasionally on campus I'd even see my dad — who was known as the Jimmy Stewart professor since he looked like the actor and had the same style of drawn-out speech and friendly delivery. Not that my dad recognized me. One day, in my first semester, I was in a crowded elevator at the library when my dad and a colleague of his walked in. "Hi!" I said enthusiastically, since this was the first time I'd seen my dad on campus. He looked at me quizzically and said, "Hi?"

I stared at him. "You don't recognize me, do you?"

"Well." He knitted his brows. "You look awfully familiar."

"Are you kidding me?"

He smiled, looking vaguely embarrassed. "I know that I know you. I just can't place the face."

"Dad!"

"Oh … Laur!" (He always called me Laur.) He chuckled. "I guess it's just out of context seeing you where I work. Or maybe your hair is different."

At this point, his Chinese colleague shook his head and said to my dad, "I recognized her and I haven't seen her in five years. And you all look the same to me!"

I laughed, which relieved all the confused people on the elevator. I wasn't offended. I was used to it. When I was in high school my friend Jane used to come over after school and liked to stop by my dad's den where he'd invariably be writing at his desk. "Hi, Dad!" she'd blurt out, imitating my voice. He'd glance up and say, "Hi, Laur, how was school today?" She'd answer that it had been okay and they'd carry on a brief conversation about homework or maybe even baseball. He never noticed that it wasn't his own offspring he was conversing with. Years later, he would learn he had facial recognition disorder, now known as face blindness. He discovered this one day when the *Globe and Mail* featured the disorder with a two-page photo spread of twelve faces, including the Queen, Brad Pitt, Bill Clinton, Madonna, Marilyn Monroe, Hitler — but the newspaper only showed those people's eyes. The celebrities were easy for the average person to recognize. My mother, myself, and my sister got them all immediately, without a second glance. But my dad didn't recognize a single one. He was truly baffled that we could recognize these people just by their eyes. All his life he'd had this peculiar condition and hadn't known it was actually a neurological affliction. It turns out that normal people use a very sophisticated part of the brain to recognize faces. But people with this disorder use a much less powerful part of the brain, the part that the rest of us use to recognize mere objects, not faces. The difference in the complexity of these two brain regions explains why we can immediately recognize people we haven't seen in ten years, but might not recognize a friend's car in our driveway, or our own suitcase at the airport. This means that for people with facial blindness, a face is just another object.

I always thought it was weird when I was a kid and my dad would say things like, "I was just out on the street and think I was talking to Leslie from next door because she was wearing glasses and Leslie wears glasses." He'd known our next-door neighbour Leslie for over a decade. Or to my sister he'd say, "I think your friend Sandy was just here asking for you." And my sister would say something like, "You mean Sandy who was here for dinner last night and who went camping with us last month?" He'd say he could tell it was Sandy because this girl talked with a lisp and Sandy has a lisp. I used to think, can't you just tell it was Sandy because it *is* Sandy? Don't you know what she looks like? But apparently he really didn't.

So, at the age of nineteen, there I was following an ambulance in which my funny, sweet, quirky dad might not be alive when we got to Toronto.

My heart was cracking in pieces, but my mother was worse. Never had she seemed so small and fragile to me. At only a hundred pounds, she'd always been a stormy force of nature, a former high school math teacher, and our household electrician, plumber, and gardener. She'd never been one to shy away from a political argument or be taken in by a vacuum cleaner salesman or a Jehovah's Witness — if she answered the door the Jehovah Witnesses would always ask for her husband instead, the one who was "always so nice." They'd never know he was a polite atheist.

At the hospital in Toronto my mother looked like the tiny person she really was. I was trying to stay strong for her, while inside I was reeling with desperation at the thought of losing my dad while still in my teens. At the administration desk, they couldn't find any record of him and we thought this meant he'd been taken to the morgue. A hellish half-hour later they figured out he was in the cardiac wing. The cardiac wing *felt* like a morgue, its long grey empty halls echoing our footsteps. Finally, we found my dad hooked up to some machines and the prognosis wasn't good. He'd had another cardiac arrest. I remember standing next to him, holding his hand, and crying while he told me, "Don't change, Laur, don't change. Just stay the way you are now."

I couldn't believe any of it was happening.

I remember as we drove through Toronto that evening to stay at my Uncle Bill's house, I stared out the window in shock at the far-too-happy people who were strolling along, holding hands, and throwing their heads back to laugh along the leafy autumn streets. I'd never felt such a stark separation from humanity before. I felt I'd crossed over some invisible line and would never be like those people out the window again, that I'd never smile again. How could they be so carefree when death was so close? Didn't they know?

Miraculously, my dad didn't die. Instead, he was told he had a year to live. Not dying that week was the best thing that ever happened to him. Every day he was thrilled to be alive. Soon after, he took early retirement and started doing things he'd been putting off: travelling, reading, writing, bird-watching, always thinking up ways to solve various world problems, and going to more baseball games — he had an uncanny knowledge of baseball, having loved the game since childhood and knowing it intimately. Anyone could ask him a random baseball question, such as, "Who played third base for Boston in 1949?" or "What happened in the fifth inning of the World Series in 1962?" and he'd always know the answer. A year after the heart incident, he was still talking baseball and politics. Then another birthday passed. Then another. He went on to live another twenty-eight years, outliving the doctor who'd given him that damning prognosis.

I think this was why when he died for real, I found that I wasn't grieving. I'd already faced his death twenty-eight years earlier. Ever since then, being with him had felt like a gift, like getting a secret glimpse into the rarely considered possibilities of what life can offer when we've almost lost it. He seemed to feel it, too. His brush with death had turned him into the most laid-back person I knew, lighter and happier than he'd ever been, always seeing how funny things were in the big picture, never letting much of anything get him down. He often said that if he died the next day he'd be okay with that, although he hoped he wouldn't. This wasn't derived from some paranormal near-death experience that made him believe in an afterlife. He just knew that life, this life on Earth, had given him a second chance.

Quinn, however, knew none of this. And at least I had been able to say goodbye to my dad, even if he'd been in a coma. Quinn hadn't. I thought of my friend's little niece who'd been there with her dog when a veterinarian euthanized the pet on the living room floor. After the dog died, the little girl folded herself against its body and emitted the saddest howl my friend had ever heard. After several minutes of wailing, she got up, wiped her tears, left the room, and was fine after that. It seemed clear to me that being part of the intimate process of death helped people cope. But as far as Quinn was concerned, his mother went away on a bus one day and when she came back his grandpa was dead. His grandpa, whom he loved so much, had been ripped from him without warning, suddenly and forever. So when Quinn sobbed at night, it was often impossible to find words to make him feel better. Telling him that I still felt like Grandpa was always around, was still with us, was still a big part of who we were, did nothing to alleviate his misery. Grandpa wasn't there physically. Quinn couldn't call him on the phone. When we visited, Grandpa wouldn't be at the door to hug us and tell us who was winning the baseball game. Quinn just couldn't grasp the finality of it all. It was as if a tidal wave of grief was forever smashing him down and he couldn't find his way to the surface. Worst were the nights when he'd cry into his pillow for forty-five minutes and suddenly become quiet. I'd think he was finally asleep. But then he'd turn to me with a tear-streaked face and red eyes and say, "Is he really dead? Really? He's *never* coming back?"

The horror of death was burying my son alive.

I started reading books on grieving children and found I could relate to something that Barbara Coloroso wrote in *Parenting Through Crisis*. She wrote that confronting the reality of death directly and honestly with children is painful at the best of times but especially today in our death-defying, cure-everything-now, fix-it-fast society and with so many of our ancestor's rituals abandoned.

I realized we'd probably made a huge mistake in not having some kind of funeral or ceremony after my dad's death. All we did was hold a memorial at my mother's house one afternoon, in which friends, family, and neighbours gathered among the seventies décor to drink white wine, eat catered sandwiches, and talk about my dad. Quinn was outside riding his unicycle most of the time, not the least interested in interacting with people he didn't know.

I thought back to places I'd visited and remembered ways people around the world dealt with death. Two years earlier, I'd travelled to Bhutan to write a story on happiness for a magazine — Bhutan is the remote Himalayan kingdom that measures its citizens' Gross National Happiness. After several days hiking on a centuries-old track through alpine wilderness, we reached a peak at close to 13,000 feet. Our guide pointed to a rocky hill beside us and explained its significance. "If a baby dies, the family brings the dead infant to the top of these rocks so vultures can take the body away. It's called sky burial." To me, a sky burial sounded appalling, but also heartbreakingly fitting. I remember gazing out at the mountain ranges all around us, and noticing that as the fast-moving clouds appeared and reappeared by the second, they revealed secret craggy peaks and shimmering green valleys for an instant before allowing them to disappear again in the fog. And then it didn't seem like such a bad place to leave a dead person after all.

I thought of Fiji where I had lived for a time in my twenties. The South Pacific islanders there, I learned, knew how to handle death and mourning. They did it communally, something Quinn hadn't experienced at all. I'd been staying with an extended Fijian family on the tiny tropical island of Taveuni, teaching school and living among the Fijians. One night, a group of us — Fijians and various backpackers who'd become friends — was circled around a beach campfire, singing, playing guitars, and drinking the traditional kava. Suddenly, we heard heart-shuddering howling coming from up the hill where the family lived. We soon learned that the patriarch of the extended family, my Fijian boyfriend's grandfather, had just died. The howling wails were coming from the women — the dead man's wife, sisters, nieces, and female cousins. These women continued to wail all night long, painful moans of deep sadness that echoed throughout the island. In the morning, a vast collection of relatives began arriving from other islands. A ten-day funeral was about to begin, a funeral that would entail two enormous feasts a day, which, incidentally, would mean a lot of women chopping vegetables on mats outside, pounding coconuts into cream, killing pigs, and a lot of people getting fat. As the boats and planes arrived, I would see women running at each other on the dirt road: sisters, cousins, and aunts who'd left Taveuni to live with their husbands' families. They'd hurl themselves into each other's arms, laughing, crying, and shrieking. The men would shake hands. The women's wailing over the dead man continued non-stop in those first several days, their passionate sobbing helping to draw the grief out of everyone. Perhaps that wailing, intense, all-consuming, unshackled, full-throated sobbing — so like Quinn's — is a natural human response to death and loss, a natural response that we North Americans have buried deep inside us. I remember thinking as I lay in my tent at night listening to the women, that although their wailing was sad it was also hauntingly beautiful, like the soul of the world revealing itself.

Oi lei! Oi lei! Ai valu! Oi lei! I can still recall it now years later.

In the days leading up to the burial in Taveuni, the body of the dead man, decorated elaborately with frangipani blossoms, was laid out in a casket in his living room. People would hover around him, kiss his cheek, and murmur their goodbyes. In the beginning, no music was allowed. Singing, dancing, even loud laughing were frowned upon by the elders for fear it would insult the ghost. Supposedly, the dead grandfather's spirit was still hovering around. It was all very sombre. On the fifth day of the funeral, however, I noticed something changing. The atmosphere seemed to be getting lighter, the wailing ebbing. People were guffawing more and they started strumming their guitars again, singing sensual Fijian harmonies deep into the night. By day seven, kids were tearing around playing hide-and-seek and racing up coconut trees. On day nine, everyone went wild. Craziness and joy seemed to unleash itself from people's hearts by the hour. Adults and kids alike started throwing buckets of water at each other, even sneaking up behind their seated-on-the-grass grandmothers for a full-body drenching, everyone screaming with hysterics. They also plastered their arms, legs, and faces with white flour. One of the regally large aunts snuck up behind me that day, put her finger to her lips and winked, then began an elaborate jiggling of her rolling-fleshed curvaceous body, all her skin white with flour like a gigantic dancing powder puff. "I'm shimmering! I'm shimmering!" she suddenly began singing out as she danced and twirled around the yard. People roared and cheered her on. The feast that night was the most enormous of all: mountains of food piled up along the woven mats outside for the hundreds of relatives gathered — fried cassava, taro, and breadfruit; fresh parrot fish in coconut cream; roasted pig cooked underground in rug-sized banana leaves. After the volumes of food that had been consumed over so many days, nobody's clothes fit any more. I remember hoping nobody would die any time soon. The island would sink from the weight. But no matter how fat we got, I realized that by the end of the ten days, the mourning had lifted. The ghost had fled.

Clearly, Fijians knew how to deal with death.

"That's it," said Rob. "We need some kind of ritual for your dad, maybe not ten days of gorging ourselves on roasted pig, but something."

He wasn't the first to suggest a ritual. Someone in Wakefield had suggested we hire a local "shaman" to perform incantations while we sat around a bonfire drumming all night. This was so far removed from anything relating to my dad that it was hard to keep a straight face. As for Quinn, I knew there was no way he could take that seriously, either. Someone else suggested that in the spring, Quinn could write a letter to his grandpa, place it in a little wooden boat, then set it off down the river, symbolically releasing him as we waved the little boat goodbye. I liked that idea better but somehow felt we needed more.

"I know," said Rob. "We could go to Toronto in June when Quinn gets out of school. We could take your dad's ashes and throw them in places around Toronto where your dad grew up, places he always talked about, like his high school track, his old neighbourhood, the woods where he went bird-watching. We could go to a Blue Jays game."

I leapt off the couch. "Rob, you're amazing! We'll call it the Grandpa Tour! And we'll throw some of his ashes on the Blue Jays field! And we'll go to the Toronto docks with the ashes, too. We'll yell *fuck off* at Lake Ontario!"

Rob gave me a quizzical look. "Swear at one of the Great Lakes?"

I reminded him of the story. My dad — who never told a lie in his life — believed he invented the English-speaking world's most widely used expletive, or at least was responsible for uniting its four-letter verb with "off." (The word *fuck* on its own likely came into existence in the fifteenth century.) In 1942, at age sixteen, my dad had a summer job as a deckhand on Lake Ontario ships alongside tough older guys who'd tease my shy young dad for never swearing. He decided to do something about it. One night lying in bed, he turned all the swear words he knew over in his head, trying out different combinations and even thinking up entirely new words that might sound dirty. Finally, after a couple of hours, the perfect phrase struck him. When he tried the expression out on the other deckhands the next morning, their jaws slacked open. They never teased him again. A year later, a strange thing happened. My dad began hearing the expression around Toronto. And it wasn't long before he began hearing the expression a lot. Decades later, when I was in my thirties, I had a friend who'd studied theatre in New York City. A group of us was discussing the origins of swear words and I mentioned this story about my dad. "Get out! You're joking!" said my friend. He told me a playwright he'd worked with in New York had written a play set during the early years of World War II. The playwright wanted a character in the play to say *fuck off*, but wanted to make sure the expression actually existed at the time his play was set. The playwright did extensive research and discovered that the term *fuck off* didn't come into common usage until 1943, and it was believed to have come from Toronto. I was flabbergasted. My dad's story held up. Sure, someone else in Toronto might have come up with the same phrase at the same time, but this seems unlikely. Ironically, I never heard my dad use the phrase himself except in telling the story. He was too nice a guy.

For the Grandpa Tour, I was already imagining how cool Quinn would think this was and how it might set free a little of his sorrow: the three of us at the Toronto docks with my dad's ashes, standing on the boardwalk by the water, letting the ashes loose into the wind as we yelled *fuck off* out at Lake Ontario. "We'll be releasing *fuck off* back to where it originated seven decades ago!"

"I love it," said Rob. "Not your everyday ritual, but who cares?"

CHAPTER 2

We were still coming up with ideas for the Grandpa Tour, planning to leave for Toronto in a few weeks, when the phone rang one morning. Rob's eighty-seven-year-old mother, Anna May, was in the hospital. She wasn't expected to survive much more than a few days.

The first thing that rushed into my mind was Quinn. How could he handle another grandparent's death when he was still so broken by the last one?

Rob took Quinn with him to the hospital in Ottawa immediately, instinctively knowing that it was the right thing to do, something I hadn't known the summer before, something I desperately wished I had known in retrospect. Quinn spent several hours that day with his soft-spoken French-Canadian "Nanny" as she hovered in and out of consciousness, hooked up to oxygen tubes.

"How did you feel about seeing Nanny today, sweetie?" I asked him that night as I tucked him into bed, the cheeping of the spring peepers in the marsh down the road coming in through the window.

"Okay. She doesn't seem too sad. She was smiling a little. And she's old."

It was true that she was, indeed, old, and had been sick and immobile in a high-care nursing home for several years. I was deeply relieved at how Quinn was taking it. Anna May spent her last day in her nursing home with a lively assortment of friends and family, including Quinn, coming in and out of her room all day. Even though they were a Catholic family, they decided against a traditional Catholic funeral. A Catholic funeral wouldn't match Anna May's undemanding, down-home, simple sweetness. Instead, they decided on a

"Celebration of Life" gathering in a room of the funeral home. I had no idea this was even possible. I thought any gathering in a funeral home meant it had to be religious. But this gathering was completely secular. Rob officiated, and, in front of his extended, close-knit, Irish-descended family, and relatives from the Gaspé, he gave the most moving eulogy I'd ever heard. He told the story of how when his mother was eight, her own mother had died. Her father, too beaten by life to care for his kids, had farmed them out to relatives. Anna May was sent to live three thousand kilometres away from the Gaspé, in a small northern Ontario fishing town where they didn't speak her native French and she didn't know a word of English. Rob recalled how strongly his mother had always felt about family because family was what she'd lost as a child.

He told the story of Anna May going to a hypnotist as an adult in hopes of losing weight. When the hypnotist asked her how old she'd been when her mother died, in her trance she'd answered, "I was eight when I died." It took a moment for those of us listening to process this statement. She hadn't told the hypnotist, "I was eight when *she* died," but, "I was eight when *I* died." Rob's voice faltered for a moment at the thought of it and he had to stop to pull himself together. "It's okay, we're with ya, bro!" called out someone in his family. "Take all the time you need!" When Rob picked up his ukulele and he and his cousin started belting out "Somewhere Over the Rainbow" in the Hawaiian ukulele-playing Israel Kamakawiwoʻole style, I wasn't the only person with tears streaming down my face in that little room with its fake wood panelling and bright yellow flowers. I looked at Quinn beside me, his hand in mine, and saw that he had tears in his eyes, too. But he was also smiling. I was so grateful that he was getting to see his dad up there openly crying in front of everyone. This is how it should be, I kept thinking. We're dealing with death as a family. This is what we missed with my dad.

I wondered if there was something primordial about grieving as a group that goes back millennia in our genes.

That afternoon at the cemetery, where Anna May was buried beside Rob's dad, Rob couldn't get words out to talk but he could sing. Over his parents' graves he sang the haunting Irish ballad "Carrickfergus" and then led us in John Prine's "Spanish Pipedream," one of Anna May's favourites that he used to sing to her. We also sang some old spirituals. I was thinking about how the music, like the Fijian women's wailing, was drawing the grief out of everyone, but lifting us up at the same time. Quinn was singing along, too. I noticed he was still wearing my dad's old silver watch. My mother had given him the watch the last time we'd visited her, two months earlier. The watch was at least thirty years old and much too big for his little wrist, but he never took it off, even wore it to school. At the burial, I noticed he kept reaching across with his other hand to touch the watch, actually tap it. I figured it must have given him comfort, thinking of his grandpa every time he felt his watch.

A few days later, I was next to him on the couch one afternoon in our living room, both of us reading. Not only was he now touching his watch more times than seemed necessary, he also seemed to be doing something I hadn't seen him do since he was six and we lived in Mexico. We called it "evening-off."

We'd lived in San Miguel de Allende for two winters and Quinn had gone to kindergarten and grade one at a Mexican Waldorf school just outside of town. While we were in Mexico, he learned Spanish from his classmates, bought tortillas on his own from our local tortilleria, and rode a rickety little bike around the narrow cobbled streets. But he also developed a strange habit in Mexico. If someone brushed his left arm by accident, he'd immediately reach up to touch his right arm, to make it even. When I saw him doing this the first time, a tingle of recognition stirred in my brain, recalling a long-forgotten memory. I remembered that when I was five and used to walk the mile to school, if I stepped on a sidewalk crack with my right foot, I would have to step on the next crack with my left foot. Otherwise it wasn't fair. I don't recall this going any further than the cracks on the sidewalks, although I do remember worrying that since I was purposely stepping on cracks I'd be breaking my mother's back, as that odd children's rhyme goes. But with Quinn, his evening-off in Mexico could get complicated, even to the point of annoying him. He would tap his left knee once, then tap his right, but then go back and tap his left knee four times, then the right knee four times. If he lost count he'd have to start all over again. I remember this going on for a couple of months in Mexico. To tease him, I'd often poke him on one arm, so he'd have to touch the other arm to even-off, which always made him laugh. One day I noticed he wasn't doing it any more. He told me he'd gotten sick of it, so stopped.

But now, four years later, he was doing it again. Only now it seemed more elaborate. As he read his book on the couch he seemed to be unconsciously tapping each elbow onto the back of the couch. Four taps of the left elbow, four taps of the right. He was also tapping the watch. A few tapless minutes would pass and then he'd start the routine all over.

"Hey, I thought you stopped evening-off in Mexico years ago. You're doing that again?" Ice was tinkling loudly in his glass of water on the coffee table.

He shrugged. "Yeah, I just like it."

"Why?"

"It's fun. It feels good."

Over the coming weeks, his evening-off became more complex, seemingly full of complicated rules. Everything had to be symmetrical and if I jokingly poked him like I used to, he'd get irritated because he'd have to embark on a highly structured system of making things even again. One day he started turning his head as far as it would go over his shoulder, then he'd have to turn his head to the other side over the other shoulder. But it didn't stop there. He'd go back and twist his head twice on the first side, then twice again on the other side. It looked like a neck exercise for old people. "Do the kids in school notice you doing that?" I asked him one day while he was building a Downton Abbey-esque estate on Minecraft, a new hobby, and TV series, he loved.

"Yeah, sometimes," he said, not looking up from my iPad.

"Don't they find it weird?"

"They just think I'm stretching my neck."

I wasn't particularly concerned. Life is a series of events that seem important at the time. When you look back sometimes you wonder why you ever worried about anything. Quinn seemed happier lately and that's all that really mattered. Perhaps the spring weather was melting some of his grief. Recently he'd come home from school excited because he'd just given a speech for his grade four class on the topic of unicycles. Afterward he'd demonstrated outside to the class how to ride one. His teacher had mentioned to me how impressed she'd been with his teaching skills. I thought, so what if he was evening-off a little? Wasn't this better than crying himself to sleep every night? Kids do strange things for short spells and then drop them all the time, just as he'd done in Mexico.

But a couple of weeks later my friend Tina and her son, Halla, came to visit from Montreal. The two boys were outside dousing each other in a water gun fight while I was making one of my raw vegan concoctions in the kitchen. Throwing some dates and pecans into the food processor, I asked Tina if she'd noticed the head turning. She shot me a look of something very close to worry. "Yeah, it's impossible not to notice. I hate to tell you, but that's not normal."

The next week we had our first pickup softball game. I'd put an ad on our online Wakefield newsgroup saying I wanted to start playing pickup softball at a nearby old diamond beside the river. "If we're hot, we'll plunge in the river after the game!" is what I'd posted. Fifteen people — both adults and kids — turned up to play ball. The air that evening was weighted down with the soft scent of lilacs, the new spring grass a supercharged luminous green I felt like rolling in. It had been a long time since I'd played softball. As for Quinn, he's athletic, but other than playing catch and batting the ball around, he'd never played an actual game, although he knew a lot about baseball from listening to my dad and watching Blue Jays games with him on TV. The village of Wakefield was different from where I grew up, where baseball and softball were part of everyday summer life. Still, Quinn took to the game that first night, getting a hit most times at bat. I was playing second base on the other team and noticed that when Quinn landed at first and waited for the next batter to hit, he started doing his neck turning. A lot. Then on second base beside me he was twisting away, then again when he reached home and stood behind the backstop. A friend of mine crinkled her brow in curiosity. "Why does Quinn keep looking over his shoulder? Is he afraid someone's going to sneak up on him?"

I laughed. "It's just something he does. No big deal."

But to myself I was thinking the real answer might be: yeah, *Death*.

CHAPTER 3

Though it is not often that Death is told so clearly to fuck off.

— Thomas Pynchon, *Gravity's Rainbow*

"You can do it, Mum," I said, "Just another twenty steps and we'll be in our seats."

It was the hottest day of the year so far, the June humidity like a living thing that tangled around you, slowing everything to a crawl as we made our way up to the nosebleed section of the stadium. The Toronto Blue Jays were about to play the Baltimore Orioles and my eighty-four-year-old mother was getting winded from all the climbing. Still, she was elated. Like my dad, she was a big Blue Jays fan. Rob couldn't join us in Toronto until the next day, so it was just the three of us for this first part of the Grandpa Tour. Soon, the game was underway.

"Keep your eyes on Bautista, Quinn," said my mother. "He's a good hitter. Oh, good, Adam Lind is coming up. Looks like Rasmus hurt his wrist...."

My mother kept throwing out comments like this and it wasn't long before the Iranian and Chinese teenagers in front of us began turning around to ask her opinion on various plays and what she thought might happen with each new batter. Quinn kept elbowing me at how funny he thought this was. He also loved that every time the smiling and bowing Japanese shortstop Kawasaki came to bat, the whole crowd would sing *Kaaaaaa-waaaaa-saki, Kawasaki, we love you, Kawasaki,* to the tune of "Yankee Doodle."

By the sixth inning, the Blue Jays were so far ahead that a lot of the Baltimore fans had given up and left, so we picked our way down closer to the field. At the seventh inning stretch, everyone rose up to sing along to the sound system's "Take Me Out to the Ball Game." I worried that the traditional song would be performed in some modern techno-style and was almost cringing as we stood. But it wasn't a techno version. What they played on the loudspeakers seemed to be an old-fashioned piano recording and the entire crowd began singing along heartily to it in the way they probably would have in the 1940s. To my surprise, I could barely get the words out to sing, my eyes brimming with tears. It wasn't just the unexpectedness of the crowd's enthusiasm for the old Tin Pan Alley tune, it was also that it was one of my dad's favourites. In fact, as I was trying to choke it out, the song swarming the cracks of my memory, I recalled that my dad had taught me all the words to it while playing catch in our backyard one night. I must have been eight or nine. *This is for you, Dad*, I kept thinking. I had the feeling that as we stood there belting out the song, my dad was right there with us, thrilled we were watching his beloved Blue Jays, grinning like a kid that they were winning by such a ridiculous lead.

The Blue Jays won 14–5, and it turned out to be the last of their eleven-game winning streak — they never made a comeback that summer. When the game was over, Quinn and I rushed down through the crowds to the front row. I pulled out a plastic container filled with some of my dad's ashes, dumped a small sand pile of them into my hand, then tossed them in the air over the field. "Enjoy the Blue Jays field, Dad!"

I looked at Quinn. He was giggling. "Do you want to try, Quinn? Throw some ashes?"

He shook his head, whipping his hands behind his back. I wasn't sure if his reluctance came from the idea of the ashes themselves, or if he was simply mortified by the open-jawed stares we were getting from nearby fans.

Either way was fine. More of the Grandpa Tour was to come.

My sister from Colorado and my cousin Kathleen joined us after the game — they weren't baseball fans. For the next part of the Grandpa Tour, I thought we'd walk around my dad's and my Uncle Bill's old neighbourhood of Baby Point Road. The sidewalks there were shaded by tall maples whose leaves that day were limp from the scorching heat. As we approached my dad's old redbrick house, I noticed Quinn on the sidewalk in front of me, hopping and jumping. He'd always liked to run and often wanted to race whoever he was walking beside, but this jumping and hopping seemed different somehow. I watched him more carefully to figure out why it was bothering me. Then I realized: he was avoiding all the cracks.

Quinn was quiet as we stood outside the house, especially when we walked around the corner to peer into the backyard from an old laneway. My cousin was describing how her dad and mine had climbed a tree that was still there, how it had been third base in their backyard games. Quinn didn't say anything but something in his face made me realize this knowledge was a little much for him, that it was too disturbingly tangible to see an actual tree my dad had climbed when he was Quinn's age. I suggested we drive around a bit, so that we could get back into the air-conditioning of my sister's rental car. Thankfully, the tour we took — to the wealthy part of the neighbourhood, Baby Point Crescent — provided an unexpected distraction. While the rest of us gaped at the multi-million-dollar mansions, Quinn started calling out, "Hey, it's a 1988 Jaguar in that driveway. And over there's a Mercedes Benz E-Class! And those people have a 2013 Porsche Panamera!" His mood had perked up. Being a car geek, he could hardly ignore exotic vehicles when he saw them.

At Runnymede Collegiate, we drove behind the school to the track where my dad had won races and the field where he had played on the football team. Quinn and I got out of the car. I'd envisioned us running around the track ourselves but it was fenced off, and besides, it was too hot to run. "I didn't think it would be like this," said Quinn, staring through the chain-link fence. "It's just a dirt track." It was true that the whole place, including the school itself, looked run-down and a little grimy, a sad echo of its former self. Clearly things had changed since the early forties. I tried to imagine my dad playing football on that field, or running around the track, perhaps talking shyly to girls. It was hard to imagine. Still, I got out some ashes and threw them over the fence. Again, Quinn didn't want to touch them. I noticed he was touching his watch, though, every time we mentioned my dad.

Our final stop that day was the Humber River Valley, at an old woods where my dad and Uncle Bill used to build forts and go bird-watching. My cousin Kathleen, along with my dad, had already scattered my uncle Bill's ashes there a few years before. Now, escaping the heat of the city, we walked into a cool and deep-green grove of deciduous forest, the dirt trail swallowing the sound of our footsteps. Quinn was on his unicycle, which he hadn't had a chance to ride since Wakefield. He zoomed ahead of us on the trail.

Immediately upon entering these woods I felt that here, more than the Blue Jays field or my dad's high school track, was where my dad's ashes should be. I think my dad felt most himself when he was outside and he had instilled in me a love of the natural world. I'd always felt at home in the woods, had grown up a stone's throw from a forest where we neighbourhood kids would spend full days playing manhunt, climbing trees, building forts, and searching for clues to solve some elaborate crime we pretended had taken place decades earlier, a secret game of ours that went on for years. On fall weekends, my dad would sometimes take us hiking to different parts of the Bruce Trail, Canada's oldest hiking trail, and when I got older I started backpacking and camping on my own. And now in Wakefield, I actually *lived* in the woods.

"I found a good place!" said Quinn, his face glowing. He had ridden back to tell us about a steep hill just ahead.

"You mean a good place for Grandpa's ashes or for you to ride down a hill?"

"Both!" he shouted back.

We followed Quinn down the trail until we came to a place where the trees were bigger, their solid trunks like an army, the branches like hands holding up the blue city sky. Warblers sang from above and I wondered if they might be descended from the same warblers that darted around here in the thirties, when my dad and uncle regularly tramped through these woods as kids with binoculars. They'd been bird-watchers — something some kids used to be back then — knowing almost as much about birds as they did about baseball, kind of like Quinn knowing the make and model of every car. I fished out containers of ashes and started passing them around. Kathleen found the exact old tree where she'd thrown her dad's ashes and we scattered some of my dad's there, too. I gazed down to where my dad's ashes were now smudging the black earth grey. Never in my life had I considered what scattering someone's ashes could actually feel like in a bone-deep way. The idea of the two brothers reuniting eight decades later in the woods of their childhood gave me a hushed feeling of joy I could store in my chest. I stood there a long time, in front of that tree, thinking about them as boys and the men they became — my genius manic-depressive uncle, the swaggering athletic historian who could hold any audience rapt by talking intelligently for hours about any decade of the past five hundred years and end by saying, *To hell with it all, I think I'll read some Yeats and then kill myself. Anyone want a Valium?* And my dad, less hip, less Kerouac-blue, but always caring toward his kid brother and always, always kinder.

When I offered Quinn a container of ashes, he shook his head no again, but didn't take off on his unicycle, either. Instead, he watched carefully as I tossed some ashes at the foot of an old wrinkled maple, a maple so sturdy and warm to the touch I imagined it had a heartbeat. I also threw some ashes around the base of a sapling nearby. "These ashes will sink into the dirt and become part of the trees. It's the cycle of life, Quinn. Grandpa will live on in this little tree, and in this old one. So a part of him will never really die."

"Really, that's true?" I turned and saw that Quinn was looking directly at me. I nodded. He held out his hand. "Can I have a container?"

Along with the container of ashes, he also took a camera and went off alone down the trail. Later that night, I saw on the camera that he'd thrown ashes around five different trees and had taken photos of each. My favourite was the photo of a tree he'd found with an ancient heart carved into it. He'd smeared ashes over the heart.

I was hoping that something had clicked in Quinn's brain that day, that an understanding about the circle of life and death on Earth had penetrated his heart, that perhaps he was finally making peace with his grandpa's death. I was crossing my fingers.

The next day we all went to Red Lobster for lunch. Along with having facial recognition disorder, my dad's taste buds also seemed to have a recognition disorder. They didn't recognize good food. Or rather, all food, even overly salty, sickly sweet, and processed food was equally delicious to my dad. A meal at Red Lobster was a big treat for him so it had to be part of the Grandpa Tour. After we consumed the chain restaurant's abundant offerings (not easy for me because I'm vegan) we snuck some of my dad's ashes into a planter on the way out. Later, I realized that although the plant looked real, it was probably plastic, which meant the dirt was also fake, which meant those ashes are still there now, and for eternity. I think my dad would find that hilarious.

The heat that day wasn't bearable for my mother and sister so they stayed at the hotel while Rob, Quinn, and I explored an exhibit of the Chinese dissident artist Ai Weiwei at Toronto City Hall. I kept noticing that Quinn was still hopping and skipping and jumping his way around the city; he was still doing the twisty thing with his neck but now he looked like he had ADHD, too. It wasn't normal for him to be so physically agitated. He was the opposite of an ADHD kid. My friend had once called him the calmest, most chilled-out, easy-going kid she'd ever met. And it had been true. As a little kid he would sit for hours playing Lego or trains by himself, wholly absorbed. But now in Toronto he was jerking his body around and throwing his limbs in every direction like a street theatre performer on speed. It was unnerving.

At Harbourfront we stood on the boardwalk overlooking Lake Ontario and saw that the setting sun was doing something orange and violet and spectacular with the air pollution. We watched the bobbing sailboats looking like toys, the lush green maples of the Toronto Islands, and the faces of the heat-bedraggled people who strolled by us or lay sprawled on the lawn.

"Are we really doing this?" whispered Quinn, eyeing the grassy slope behind us. "There's a lot of people. What will they think?"

"Who cares?" I said, looking around, secretly a little gun-shy now that the moment was here. I dug into my bag for more ashes. When we each had our handful, we hesitated, getting up our nerve.

"On three," said Rob. We counted, slowly. Finally, we threw our arms up in the air, letting loose the thousands of tiny grey-white pebbles that were my dad. They soared skyward, arced over the lake, and got caught in the breeze as we shouted, "Fuck off!" louder and with more gusto than we'd ever shouted it.

Returning the phrase back to its birthplace.

People gaped. We started laughing, even a little hysterically. Quinn was laughing the hardest. That's when he asked for more ashes. So he could throw them on his own.

CHAPTER 4

Shortly after returning to Wakefield, I got an email from a photographer who happened to take Quinn's picture while we were in Guelph after the Grandpa Tour. He'd been hired as the official photographer for a downtown event involving modern dancers performing in Guelph's fountain splash pad, followed by a concert where the audience had danced in the water too. This photographer had happened to see a kid riding a unicycle that night and thought it would make a good shot. When I looked at the picture in my email, I couldn't help noticing Quinn touching his watch even though he was riding his unicycle. I knew he'd been doing this since Rob's mother's burial, but I'd tried to dismiss it, telling myself it wasn't a big deal. But now it had even been captured digitally and I couldn't ignore it any more. What was going on with all his strange new behaviours and the evening-off?

Lying in bed with my tablet that warm summer night, I decided to Google, "kids making things even" to see what came up. I doubted I'd get anything since those words together seemed so arbitrary, so unusual. But I was shocked to find link after link with that very phrase, including a link that led to something called "symmetry rituals." A crack in my brain started to form. Symmetry rituals. That's exactly what Quinn was doing, performing rituals so everything was symmetrical on both sides of his body. Like my stepping on the sidewalk cracks. I found a forum where a teenage girl was describing how if she tapped her left forearm, she'd have to tap her right forearm. It was getting too complicated and distracting, she said, and her friends at school were starting to think it was weird. I couldn't believe the words I was reading. This was just like Quinn. How could something so seemingly random and bizarre be so ubiquitous? People's brains were forcing them to do this curious thing they felt they simply *had* to do. It wasn't just my own kid making everything "even" but enough people that there were entire websites about it. I looked up at the url of one of the websites and inhaled a deep startled breath. It was a website for obsessive compulsive disorder.

Next I came across a test from the OCD Center of Los Angeles, which had a checklist to ascertain whether or not your child might have obsessive compulsive disorder. I scanned the list. The first five traits dealt with cleanliness, hand washing, and compulsive tidying of bedrooms. Quinn's hands were almost always dirty. I was forever reminding him to wash them before eating. As for his bedroom, the floor was a landmine of Legos, toy cars, and Archie comics. But the sixth trait jumped off the page at me: "If my child does things on one side of his/her body, he/she often needs to do a similar action on the other side in order to make things "equal," or "even," or "symmetrical."

Could Quinn have OCD? I barely knew what OCD was but I knew I'd be spending the rest of the day and many days to come finding out. Within that very hour I learned that OCD is anxiety-related, often genetic, and, in children, can be triggered by trauma: parental divorce, bullying, the death of a loved one. My heart lurched. Death of a loved one. I went on to read that many kids can have mild OCD tendencies, as perhaps I'd had with the sidewalks and Quinn had had in Mexico. But with me it had withered and disappeared, as I thought it had with Quinn, back in Mexico, though I didn't know then that it was OCD. But all along it had been there inside him, waiting to uncoil and rear its serpent head if it got the chance.

And to think I'd been relieved lately that Quinn's nightly crying into his pillow had subsided. It had reminded me of when he was an infant and I noticed one day his incessant crying from colic had miraculously stopped. Suddenly I had a smiling quiet baby instead of one we had to wrap in a towel and duct-tape to the top of the warm, rumbling dryer to get him to stop crying and sleep. And now, years later, I had made myself believe that the Grandpa Tour had eased something in his troubled mind. At what point, I wondered, did his mournful crying morph into OCD? Was it a single indecipherable instant or was it more gradual, like the day you realize that one season has finally surrendered to another and you didn't see it happen? Somehow his winter of sorrow had silently slipped into his spring of OCD. Why had he stopped crying for his grandpa and started instead to want everything to be balanced, even, to feel just right? Lately, he'd started a new behaviour in which every time he entered a room, he'd knock his elbow against each of the four walls, to make things even. Was it a chemical change in his brain, searching to control the uncontrollable? Perhaps death had simply been too overwhelming for his young mind to contemplate and his brain had found these behaviours the best available coping mechanism for unfathomable loss, loss that triggered fears about future losses and his inability to prevent them. Was he physically saving himself from drowning in his own grief?

A thousand thoughts tumbled around in my skull.

CHAPTER 5

Everyone was lined along the riverbank waiting for it to appear. Since it was July 1, the sun was blinding as we gazed over the shimmering water, and making out a ramshackle pirate ship in the distance wasn't easy. But then some kid shouted, "There it is!" and everyone squinted harder. The kid was right. The Wakefield Raft, constructed new and more creatively every year by the village teens, was sailing down the Gatineau River toward us, just as the Canada Day Parade was starting behind us. Already we heard drumming and singing from the floats, and, as always, leading the parade on his upright red bicycle was the lovely older man known to all in Wakefield as the Village Poet. As every year, a chicken tea cozy adorned the Village Poet's head. The Wakefield Granny float was next, filled with a dozen laughing grandmothers who had started an international movement to support grandmothers taking care of AIDS orphans in Africa. Next came the SOS float where they were shouting, "Save our Spring!" As a member myself, we'd been trying to protect the town's source of spring water, and our mock funerals, marches, and benefits were popular, almost as much as the Save Our River rallies to stop a septic sludge plant from polluting the river. Wakefielders had won that fight and the Gatineau River had been saved, and now the teenagers on the pirate ship were plunging from the top deck straight into the river's chilly blue depths. We all cheered for the kids, for the river, for Wakefield.

"There's Quinn!" I called to Rob a few minutes later. Quinn was riding his unicycle in the parade, weaving in and around the floats. I barely had time to look up to wave at him because I'd set up an iced cappuccino stand on the sidewalk. Just when Quinn passed, I was inundated with thirsty parade goers.

Quinn was still wearing, and habitually touching, my dad's watch, and still evening-off, but other than that, it seemed his OCD was waning. I was thinking that if he did have OCD, it was mild.

A week or so after Canada Day, we visited my friends Kevin and Jack in Northumberland County to help them add a wing to their straw bale home. Quinn had so much fun threading the long needles with twine and then through the haystacks, and riding on tractors, that his OCD was virtually nonexistent that weekend. I wondered if it would soon disappear entirely.

"Look, Mummy, I stopped!" It was August and Quinn had just returned from two weeks of summer camp. Standing in our open doorway, the pine-scented air of the sultry summer night rushing in with him, he reached up to touch his left cheek. "See?"

He didn't reach for the other cheek.

"Did you notice? I'm over it. I don't need to even-off any more!" He threw himself at me for a long hug and I breathed in deeply the campfire smell of his hair.

"That's fantastic, Quinn! I'm so happy for you! I missed you!"

Rob had been right. I'd been worrying too much. I could put away all those books about OCD that I'd been reading. Somehow, he'd gotten over OCD on his own, at camp. Relief flowed through my every vein.

Until the next morning, when I tried lifting his backpack off the floor. "Quinn, this backpack weighs more than you do. What's in here, rocks?"

"Yeah, maybe a few," said Quinn, distractedly, as he tied his shoelaces to go out and ride his bike.

"I was kidding. You actually have rocks in here?" When I looked inside, I felt a catch in my chest. Rocks of all sizes filled the pack to the brim. "I don't get it. These aren't colourful or interesting shapes. They're just boring grey rocks. Can we throw them outside?"

"No!" Quinn launched himself protectively on top of the pack. "I collected them all at camp. I'm never letting them go! I can't!" He gave me a fierce pleading look, one I didn't recognize on him at all. I stared back at him. A different sort of rock had just lodged itself in my stomach.

I tried to let it drop, but it seemed too much like hoarding, afraid of letting things go. Wasn't that another OCD tendency? Also, he was wearing my dad's watch again. He hadn't taken it to camp, preferring to keep it safe in a box somewhere only he knew about in his bedroom. At breakfast he'd told me that when he'd been lonely at camp, he'd think of the hidden watch in its special box and it had made him feel less lonely. It reminded me of an autobiography I'd read years earlier called *Memories, Dreams, Reflections* by the psychiatrist Carl Jung. When Jung was about Quinn's age he'd carved a little man out of a wooden ruler. He gave this little "manikin" a bed, a coat, and a special painted stone, and placed the manikin in a pencil case. Jung wrote:

> Secretly I took the case to the forbidden attic at the top of the house (forbidden because the floorboards were worm-eaten and rotten) and hid it with great satisfaction on one of the beams under the roof — for no one must ever see it! I knew that not a soul would ever find it there. No one could discover my secret and destroy it. I felt safe, and the tormenting sense of being at odds with myself was gone. In all difficult situations, whenever I had done something wrong or my feelings had been hurt, or when my father's irritability or my mother's invalidism oppressed me, I thought of my carefully bedded-down and wrapped-up manikin and his smooth, prettily colored stone.

It made sense that there was something comforting in secreting away a treasure in a box, and that in thinking of the hidden watch when he was lonely, Quinn was keeping safe his connection to his grandpa. Yet, when he wore the watch now, I kept seeing glimpses of him whispering to it. I just couldn't catch what he was saying.

A couple of days later I went to see a concert at the Black Sheep Inn in Wakefield, a popular bar where well-known Canadian musicians play. I happened to be standing near the back when a woman I recognized asked me how I was. Sometimes it's comforting to pour your heart out to a stranger, so over the blaring of the singing and drums I ended up telling her my worries, explaining that my son was having trouble letting go of his grandpa. She asked his name, then the name of my dad. It seemed an odd line of questioning. When I told her their names, she touched my arm, looked meaningfully into my eyes, and said, "I'm picking up something here. Spirit is telling me something about them."

"Spirit?" I shouted. The music had gotten louder.

"Spirit."

She spoke in a voice that echoed with deep knowledge. I couldn't help myself, so I asked loudly, "Do you mean *a* spirit? I think *spirit* needs an indefinite article." I grinned, trying to be friendly.

She held her open hands up to either side of her mouth to direct her voice. "They had a past life together!" She raised her eyebrows and nodded knowingly, then reached into her pocket to give me her card, adding that I could book a session with her. Smiling politely, I turned my attention back to the band. When I glanced at the card the next day, it said something about past life channelling, or energy healing, or some combination of the two, and I crumpled it into the trash. A few days later I happened to see her again while I was riding my bike to the bakery. She bee-lined across the street when she spotted me so that she could tell me something that seemed urgent. "Spirit told me more about your son and your dad. It was a native voice that told me. The voice told me about a native animal. That's their connection, your dad and son. I'm feeling your son has a strong connection to animals?"

An orange VW van chugged past as I thought about this. "Actually, no. It's kind of weird but he's not interested in animals at all. He got bitten and barked at by some big dogs on our street as a little kid, that could be why."

"Oh." She looked downcast.

"He likes vehicles."

"Vehicles?"

"Cars mostly. I don't know why."

"Your dad then. He must have had a connection to animals."

I squinted out at the river and thought about this also. "Nope. He liked baseball. And he was a traveller. A geographer, too. Oh, he *was* a bird-watcher."

"Well, there you go! That must be what I was picking up. Birds. I gave you my card, right?"

"Yep," I said, starting to pedal and make my getaway. As I rode, I thought, *native* animal? Weren't all wild animals around here roaming the continent for eons before any humans showed up? I thought Spirit must have been confused.

Two days later, my university friend Shazea and her family arrived. Even though Shazea had moved to Spain over twenty years earlier, and then to England, where she'd married an Englishman, we'd always stayed friends, although mostly by writing. We didn't get to see each other often enough. I'd visited her in Spain, and then stayed with her in London when my first book was short-listed for an award, and then again a few years later for a book tour, and she'd visited Canada a few times. Part of the reason she was coming this time was because she's a gifted poet and a book of hers had just been published. She'd be giving some readings while in Canada. Shazea and I had a lot to catch up on. We were both mothers now with busy lives, although it was a different kind of busy than we'd been at university, when we'd stay up all night to finish a history or English essay, then stay up again the next night to crash a downtown party, always hoping to meet interesting cute guys but usually failing at that. Looking back I realize it was because we were probably too shy, or not looking in the right places, but our excuse was that we always wanted to make it home — hitchhiking or double-riding on my mountain bike — by 1:00 a.m. to watch a Mary Tyler Moore rerun on our tiny TV. She called me Mary and I called her Rhoda. Or maybe it was the other way around.

In any case, life wasn't like that any more.

We took Shazea and her husband, Bill, and the kids to the National Art Gallery in Ottawa where the highlight for the kids was lying back in a darkened room on beanbag chairs and gazing up at abstract art swirling around on the ceiling while throaty-voiced Icelandic music played. Afterward, we ate shawarma and falafel on the front lawn of the Parliament buildings while watching something called "The Sound and Light Show," which was a lot more entertaining than it sounds.

The best part would be our upcoming camping trip to Giant Caterpillar Island. Rob, Quinn, and I had been going to this little island for the past three years and had named it ourselves, although I'm sure everyone who goes there has a different name for the place. For three years in a row on the island we'd seen a single enormous caterpillar lumbering along a giant granite rock, a creature the same length and girth as Rob's middle finger. One year, I'd taken a photo and put it on Facebook to see if anyone knew what it was, and someone had recognized it as the caterpillar of an imperial moth. The moth is apparently the size of an adult's spread-out hand. One day, I'd love to see that moth emerge.

To reach the island, all we had to do was strap a canoe to the top of our Toyota Echo, drive half an hour north along the Gatineau River, park the car at a boat launch north of the dam, dump the canoe into the river, and load it with our camping gear. From there, it was a forty-five-minute paddle to the island, which, on weekdays, was always deserted. Since the river is dammed, the water there is more like one of the nearby vast Canadian Shield lakes, blindingly blue and dotted with emerald-green islands jam-packed with conifers, massive white pines emerging from the canopy like lone jade stars, and craggy cliffs perfectly designed for jumping into the water.

Even though Shazea had grown up in Canada she had never really camped before, and Bill, an actor with the Royal Shakespeare Company who'd lived in London most of his life, definitely hadn't. He could hardly wait to see Canada's wild side after what they'd seen of the urban sprawl of southern Ontario, before visiting us.

Because of the heat on the day we left, the river seemed draped in an impressionist haze, but once we'd paddled a bit and got out in the breeze, the air became a reverie of wistful summer memories, pungent with cedar. Not only were Shazea and her family with us but so was my friend Tina and her son, Halla. Halla and Quinn had been buddies for years and ever since Halla and his mother had moved to Montreal from Wakefield, the boys had missed each other. Now they'd get to spend a week on the island together. Since there were so many of us we'd borrowed extra canoes and kayaks from our neighbours and everyone seemed to be getting the hang of paddling through the choppy water. As we made our way to the island, I felt an uprush of happiness.

I looked over at Quinn, who was paddling a kid's kayak. He seemed completely himself, giggling with Halla, not doing anything OCDish. Gradually, I thought, the rock of grief in his heart was being chipped away. Maybe this camping trip would finally set him completely free of it. I looked up at the Wizard of Oz sky of endless blue, felt the afternoon light pouring down on us all, and watched Giant Caterpillar Island come into view around a bend.

I had no way of knowing how ephemeral the moment was, that the coming days on the island would be the last pulse of an uncomplicated serenity that we wouldn't know again for a long time to come.

We never did see the giant caterpillar on that trip. However, by the end of four days, all of us were regularly taking running leaps off the highest ledge of rock into the water. On one of the lower ledges, I'd even done a back dive, something I hadn't tried since my teens. Everyone had to leave on the fourth day, except for me, Quinn, and Halla, who'd get to stay another three days. This turned out to be my favourite time.

We were in the middle of a heat wave — it had been a whole summer of heat waves — but on the island we hardly noticed because we'd spend the day in our bathing suits and throw ourselves off the jumping rock whenever we felt hot, the water enveloping our bodies like cool silk. At night the echo of loons pierced the air with an ancient laughter. During the long afternoons, while I read in a hammock, Quinn and Halla carved sticks into daggers, did cannonballs off the jumping rock to see who could make the biggest splash, laughed at the way I jumped because it reminded them of a cave woman, played an endless card game of War, paddled the canoe around the island, read comics, and poked at the campfire. Shazea had left us a pack of coloured origami paper and shown us how to make paper frogs. I didn't think the boys would be interested in this but it turned out that a week on an island is just the thing for making origami frogs. The boys must have made fifty of them each. They even gave the frogs names and invented some kind of world for them. I noticed a lot of those frogs met their demise in the campfire.

"Laurie," Halla said to me hesitantly one morning when Quinn was still in the tent, "does Quinn actually eat sticks and pebbles or does he just carry them around in his mouth?"

I gaped at him. *What the hell?*

"Oh, never mind," he added after seeing my face. "He must just be carrying them around in his mouth for fun. Maybe I'll try it, too."

It was such a sweet and loyal response that I felt a surge of love for Halla, wondering if he really did think it was just a game. I didn't mention anything to Quinn about his latest habit of popping sticks and stones in his mouth, but I kept my eye on him.

On the evening we left and paddled back toward civilization, we were surrounded by a dazzle of light on the water. The sun had set and the colours were soft and muted, spreading gauze-like around us as the night's darkness seemed gradually to lift out of the river. In the last ambient light that remained, I thought I saw something moving in the water just off the edge of our canoe. At first it looked like two jumbles of sticks but I soon realized it was antlers. "Look," I whispered to the boys, "a deer!" Aloof to the human world, this magnificent creature was completely silent as it glided along through the dark water. We barely dipped our paddles in, not wanting to alarm it. My heart stirred as I felt like a kid who'd come across a secret presence from another time. I'd seen plenty of deer in my life — they regularly visited our yard in the winter — but had never seen one swimming right beside me through the dark.

"Cool!" whispered Quinn and Halla. "Does it know we're here?"

I had no idea but gave a whispered thanks to the animal for unintentionally bestowing us with this gift. In the weeks to come, I'd think back to that deer and ache to be in its tranquil, hushed world again.

CHAPTER 6

Once we returned to Wakefield, Quinn looked at the calendar and realized how few days he had left before school began. Most kids mildly dread the end of summer vacation, but Quinn seemed overly troubled by the thought of returning to school. I found it puzzling. He'd never minded much before.

One night as we sat down to dinner, I caught him taking what looked like a leaf out of his mouth before starting to eat.

"Now you're eating leaves, too?" I asked. "This is entertaining. I can't wait to see what weird thing you'll do next." Quinn gave me a quizzical look and burst out laughing. Next, he dropped to the floor and started licking the carpet, giggling the whole time.

"Okay, that's pretty weird. It's even more bizarre than storing rocks in your mouth." I spooned rice onto his plate and looked down at my son, who had his face in the carpet. "Maybe don't try that one at school," I added. He fell into further fits of hilarity, rolling on the floor, then stood up to lick the window pane. "Hey, that's new. Good one!"

Quinn kept laughing. At least he finds his OCD amusing, I thought. "Quinn, this is reminding me of a story I read about a kid who licked light switches at school."

After dinner, I found the story I was looking for, "A Plague of Tics" by essayist David Sedaris, and read it to Quinn. It's a true story about the obsessive compulsive behaviour that plagued Sedaris's life from elementary school all the way to college. He'd lick every light switch he encountered and count all 637 steps walking home from school, pausing every few feet to "tongue a mailbox," and stopping to lick a neighbour's concrete mushroom lawn ornament on the way, hoping its guardian wouldn't rush out from her house shouting at him to get his face out of her toadstool. He described how he was compelled to do these things because nothing was worse than the anguish of not doing them. He wrote that he hated his mind, that there must be an off-switch somewhere but he was damned if he could find it.

Quinn didn't seem to like the story as much as I did. "I kind of get what he was doing but I'm not like that," he said, kicking his soccer ball against a wooden step in the living room.

Kicking the soccer ball was fine, but I noticed he'd been kicking imaginary monsters behind every door whenever he entered a room.

"No, you're not," I agreed. But secretly I wasn't so sure.

EMAIL, LATE AUGUST 2013

Hi Tina,

I'm worried about Quinn again. Now he can't fall asleep unless one of us is in his room. The other day he was licking the carpet and for a while now I've noticed he has been eating dirt and twigs. Every day he seems to do a new wacky thing. He mutters to himself every night and lately has to touch the wall when he's doing it. I don't know what to do. I think he needs therapy but I wouldn't have a clue what kind. He's traumatized by my dad's death. He just can't get over it. Yesterday I walked into the office and in the middle of the floor was my iPad and on the iPad was a photo of my dad that he'd found online. He'd just left it there for me to see. I'm so worried about him that I'm having trouble sleeping.

Laurie

Oh, Laurie,

It sounds like Quinn definitely needs to talk to someone. Will you go to a pediatrician for a referral or something? Now I understand what Halla was talking about when he said that Quinn was eating rocks on the island. I said, "What? Surely he wasn't actually eating them, though." And he said, "Well, he was carrying them around in his mouth." Do you think he might be performing rituals with the subconscious hope that it might somehow magic his grandpa back? Sort of like a dare? Like if he does something outrageous, maybe things will be different somehow? I don't mean that he's doing it in a conscious way, of course. Or maybe he's just trying to keep himself busy so that he doesn't think about the pain of losing him, something novel to distract him from his grief. I don't know. But I really feel for him. Sweet little guy. God knows we all have our own weird shit.

Tina

The night before school started, Quinn was lying next to me but not paying attention as I read him a Percy Jackson book. He seemed lost in his own world, mumbling unintelligible words to himself, or perhaps, to the watch, and repeatedly touching the watch and then touching his heart.

"Quinn, what's the matter, sweetie?"

He sighed. "I just don't want to go to school. I want summer to keep going."

I reached out to tousle his newly cut hair. "But you'll get to see your friends. You'll play soccer every day at recess. And you might get that nice teacher Mr. DeFranco."

"I know, but what if I don't?"

"Try not to worry about it. Since when did you become such a worrier?"

"I just miss Grandpa." There was a choke in his voice as tears sprang to his eyes, making them instantly rimmed with red.

As I tried to comfort him I felt my heart floundering around my chest. OCD wasn't so funny any more. And this crying was like time curving back to those dark days of grief.

Quinn did get the nice teacher, Mr. DeFranco, and I thought things would pick up once he got into the regular routine of school. They didn't, though. Every night at bedtime I was accompanied by a child I barely recognized. Instead of listening with rapt attention to my reading, as he'd done all his life, he'd be on the extreme edge of the bed, tense and fidgety, mumbling what sounded like incantations. Finally, I asked him what he was saying.

In a small, faraway voice he started to explain: "When I was at camp I cried about Grandpa a lot, so the camp counsellors told me I should talk to him. That's when I started doing it, talking to Grandpa."

I swallowed, trying to keep my voice calm. "You're talking to Grandpa?"

He nodded.

"What do you say to him?"

"I ask him to come back."

A cold finger was laid on my insides. I thought about Tina's email. Quinn was staring at one of his car posters on the wall, not looking at me. After a moment, I said, "You what?"

"If I say "come back" ten times while I touch my watch I think he'll really come."

"And all the other stuff you do? That's all to bring Grandpa back, too?"

He turned to me, eyes wide, and gave me a single solemn nod. "Oh sweetie, that's just … magical thinking. People don't come back from the dead, no matter how many times you touch your watch. You can talk to Grandpa and tell him you miss him and tell him about your day, but Grandpa isn't coming back."

The tears that had been swelling up behind his eyes suddenly erupted. He turned away from me to cry against the wall.

Good God, I thought, what was I dealing with?

"Quinn, listen to me," I said, rubbing his back. "We're going to figure this out together. I'll look at those OCD books again. They can help us. They have exercises we can do. To change the patterns in your brain. This isn't you. It's a hiccup in your brain, like a computer glitch we can fix. You won't be stuck with this OCD bully in your head forever. I promise."

Quinn turned to face me, taking in my words, hanging on to them like a life raft it seemed. He took a deep breath. I thought he was rallying a little.

It felt like we were in for a long battle.

CHAPTER 7

Obsessive compulsive disorder is a neurobiological condition affecting three in every one hundred people. It's more prevalent than diabetes but talked about much less. Until recently, the prognosis was dire, the condition misunderstood as a kind of neuroses. With OCD, the part of the brain that filters information isn't functioning properly, causing certain thoughts — thoughts that should be forgotten — to get stuck. It's as if the person is trapped by an unrelenting heckler or bully who throws out jabs of worry, fear, and uncertainty. In Quinn's case, it seemed his bully was saying, "If you touch your watch and ask Grandpa to come back ten times, he will. If you don't do it, he won't come back. If you keep all these rocks, he'll come back. If you let the rocks go, you'll never see him again." Children have no idea what's going on when they start to experience intrusive thoughts and compulsions. The obsessions and compulsions can take over their waking hours. The obsessions themselves are persistent, unwanted thoughts or images that intrude into a child's thinking and cause anxiety. Compulsions are covert mental acts or behaviours performed repetitively to relieve or prevent the worry or anxiety generated by the obsession, and they're often intended to magically prevent some dreaded event. Quinn's case seemed a bit different, in that his obsession was his grandpa coming back to life, and his compulsions were to make that happen. In the reading I'd done, the compulsions were almost always to *prevent* something bad from happening. For instance, a child washing her hands over and over thinks the hand washing will prevent her from getting a dreaded disease. Quinn's compulsions were to bring about something good. However, when I looked at it another way, by not doing the compulsions, his worst fear would be realized: his grandpa would never come back. From everything I'd read, the more you give in to the compulsions the more the bully tells you to keep obeying them and the more entrenched the neural pathways become. The more you feed it, the more it wants, demanding ever-increasingly unreasonable demands. OCD never gets enough.

Thankfully, though, I was relieved to discover that with advances in brain science, wherein scientists have learned that the brain isn't rigid and unchangeable but malleable and "plastic" (the science of neuroplasticity) a revolution has taken place. OCD and conditions like it can be treated with cognitive behaviour therapy. Dr. Jeffrey Schwartz, author of *Brain Lock: Free Yourself from Obsessive-Compulsive Behavior,* writes about how they now have scientific evidence that cognitive behaviour therapy can actually cause chemical changes in the brains of people with OCD. He says that by changing your behaviour, you can change your brain chemistry, free yourself from what he calls "brain lock," and finally get relief from OCD's debilitating symptoms.

So when I told Quinn that we could fix the glitch in his brain and change his brain patterns through exercises, I was serious. I'd spent long nights researching OCD and learning about the wonders of cognitive behaviour therapy. I'd ordered books on Amazon, such as *What To Do When Your Brain Gets Stuck: A Kid's Guide to Overcoming OCD, Talking Back to OCD,* and *Freeing Your Child from Obsessive-Compulsive Disorder.* The author of the last book, Dr. Tamar Chansky, affirmed my belief that OCD can be low-grade in many children, but a traumatic event, such as a family death, can tip the scales and cause the OCD to become full-blown. Full-blown. I didn't think Quinn's OCD was full-blown. I was hoping we were nipping it in the bud.

When I explained to Quinn that OCD was like a bully in his brain that bossed him around, I told him to boss the bully back, that the bully only had power if Quinn gave it power, that the bully was like the man behind the curtain in the *Wizard of Oz.* He was only powerful because people thought he was. Really, he was just an ordinary man behind a curtain, not a wizard at all.

One day Quinn came home from school and told me he'd beaten his OCD. It was the day I'd made an appointment for him to see our family doctor the next week. "I told the bully to fuck off," he said proudly. Except for the throwing of the ashes into Lake Ontario, I never thought I'd be so happy to hear my son use that phrase. Unfortunately, the next school day, a Friday, wasn't so easy for him. Quinn came home in tears. His OCD bully had returned, although he wouldn't tell me how.

An idea flashed in my head. Rob was playing soccer that night but Quinn and I were free. "I know, Quinn," I said. "You and I should take our own little road trip in the camper van. We could pack and leave right now."

An hour later we were on the road north to a town called Maniwaki. I'd never been there — we always seemed to drive south, west, or east from Wakefield, never very far north — but I'd been curious about Maniwaki ever since we'd moved to Wakefield. I thought Quinn and I could explore the town, see a movie, and find a place to camp. The advantage of a camper van is that you can pretty much park it anywhere and nobody knows you're in there sleeping. As we drove along the highway, I could smell the crispness of a thousand drying leaves. Already, sumacs glistened cinnamon red and an orange flotilla was spiralling out of the sky, ushering autumn in like an unwelcome guest. I was never ready for summer to go.

On the two-hour drive north, I was reminded that our camper van is a gas guzzler, something I'd always known but that, with the out-of-control gas prices, was now painfully obvious, and I learned that there is nothing whatsoever of interest on the drive north to Maniwaki. When we arrived in the town itself, I realized it was even less interesting than the drive.

"This is an ugly, boring town," noted Quinn. It was hard to argue. But at least we could watch a movie. A website had told us that Maniwaki had a movie theatre and listed which current movies were showing. But strangely, we couldn't find the theatre. When we went to a library to ask where it was, the librarian said, "That theatre burned down a long time ago."

"But there's a website. It says what movies are playing there tonight." I could hear pleading in my voice. So far this road trip was tanking fast. She shrugged, then told us to try a bigger town farther north called Mont-Laurier. They had a movie theatre that hadn't burned down. We decided to give it a try.

The drive to Mont-Laurier was more appealing because, on the way, we seemed to cross some invisible line into truly wild country. A big black bear sauntered across the lonely deserted highway right in front of us. I didn't see a single building anywhere, just endless rolling hills of dense forest and lakes. When we reached the town, which seemed like a mini Mont Tremblant, full of ski equipment shops, we asked directions to the theatre at a pharmacy. Nobody spoke English so I made Quinn ask in French, which mortified him. Normally he's a little shy but this shouldn't have been a big deal. He was rapidly losing confidence in himself. When we found the theatre, all the Hollywood movies were dubbed into French, so we decided just to get something to eat and find a place to sleep that night. It was while we were driving to find a camping spot that Quinn asked what time it was. I said it was around 9:30.

"What? I missed eight o'clock!" Quinn sounded almost hysterical.

I looked over at him in the dark. In the light from the dashboard I could see that his face had crowded into the features of a frightened kitten. "What do you mean? What happens at eight o'clock?"

"That's when I talk to Grandpa every night. That's why I go outside then. That's when I ask him to come back!" His eyes shone in alarm as tears began to river down his face.

Things didn't improve that evening. At the place we camped, a little cul-de-sac beside a brook where crickets chirped in the branches just outside our window, Quinn kept getting out of the van. He had a different excuse every time. He wanted to look at the stars. He wanted to walk around. It was too hot in the van. Every time he left I overheard him out there talking and, at one point, singing. I knew he was trying to communicate with my dad, trying to make up for having missed talking to him at eight o'clock. When he finally came to bed, he couldn't settle down. At one point he got up and started jumping, trying to stay suspended in the air.

"Why are you doing that?" I asked. Even though it was funny, I wasn't laughing. It was obvious he was miserable.

"I just am."

"But why?"

He collapsed down on the bed. "To get closer to Grandpa."

CHAPTER 8

OCD floods its victims with invasive thoughts and behaviours guided by various rules that can change daily. A new behaviour I'd started noticing was that Quinn had to leave a room by the exact route he'd entered it, sometimes even walking backward, retracing his steps. This in itself wasn't any more peculiar than his other seemingly random and baffling behaviours, but what I found intriguing was that this new one, like the evening-off, seemed to be so common for people with OCD. Quinn called it erasing. According to the OCD Foundation, erasing, cancelling, and undoing are all common OCD compulsions.

For Quinn, everything had to go back to zero, to be symmetrical. On an online OCD forum, a teenager had written that he's always late for class because it's complicated negotiating the hallways when he has to walk back the same way he'd come before he could proceed to another place. A mother wrote about her son having to "backtrack incessantly" wherever he went, even forcing her once to exit from a parking lot the same way she'd come in. I wondered what was happening in the inner workings of people's brains. Did this evening-off, this need for symmetry, somehow go back in our evolutionary history? And if so, why? None of my books on OCD discussed this, and neither could I find anything online. It wasn't until I happened to read a book on a completely different topic — what makes things compelling — that I found a possible answer. I was reading a fascinating book called *Riveted: The Science of Why Jokes Make Us Laugh, Movies Make Us Cry, and Religion Makes Us Feel One with the Universe,* by the cognitive scientist Jim

Davies, and came across a section where he discusses symmetry. He wrote that being able to detect patterns in the world has been crucial to our survival. In the natural world, being able to pick out the face of a living thing hiding in the forest could save your life. Faces of living things — be they humans, snakes, cougars, or wolves — are symmetrical. We're programmed to pay attention to symmetry, to be on alert for things being even. I almost dropped the book on the floor as I read that. Finally, I had an answer for why Quinn, and even my five-year-old self with the sidewalk-crack-stepping, might be so compelled to want things to be even and symmetrical. And not only are we always looking for existing patterns, our brains have adapted to see patterns where no patterns actually exist.

Michael Shermer, the American science writer and author of over a dozen books, including *The Believing Brain: From Ghosts and Gods to Politics and Conspiracies — How We Construct Beliefs and Reinforce Them as Truths*, asks you to imagine you're walking home across the grasslands in Africa three million years ago. You hear a rustle nearby. Is it the wind or a predator? If you assume it's a predator and it turns out to be just the wind, you've made a Type I Error in cognition, a false positive, believing something is real when it isn't. You've found a nonexistent pattern and no harm is done. You steer clear of the rustling noise, now more alert, and find another path home. But what if you assume the rustle in the grass is only the wind when it's actually a predator? This is a Type II Error in cognition, a false negative. You're not believing something is real when it is, in this case a predator. Too bad for you, you're dead, no longer a member of the gene pool. Our brains are belief engines that have evolved to recognize patterns. We connect the dots and create meaning from patterns we think we see in nature. Sometimes one dot really is connected to another dot and sometimes it isn't. The baseball player who always taps his bat on the plate three times before he hits a home run forms a false association but it's not a life-threatening one. But when the association is real, we learn something about our surroundings to help us survive. We are descended from those early hominoids who were most successful at finding patterns. This is called *patternicity*, the tendency to find meaningful patterns in both meaningful and meaningless noise. The problem is that figuring out the difference between a Type I and Type II error is difficult, especially when a split second could determine life or death in our early ancestors' environment. Therefore, the default is to assume all patterns are real, in other words, that all rustles in the grass are predators. According to Shermer, this mental process is the basis for all superstition and magical thinking. For those with OCD, this primal tendency of being hyperaware of patterns is, for some reason, in overdrive. It's an adaptive behaviour — one that has kept our species alive — gone rogue. Stephen Whiteside, a psychologist at the Mayo Clinic, has said that OCD activities done in typical levels can be helpful. Jim Davies, in *Riveted*, agrees, saying that OCD is probably the result of overactivity of mental processes that normally help us. For example, keeping clean and staying away from germs are practices that are good for us.

We had a busy weekend planned toward the end of September. One of Rob's cousins was getting married and we'd been invited to the wedding in Ottawa. Before that, we'd be driving to Montreal to buy a car we'd found on Kijiji. On the way to Montreal, Quinn kept rolling down his window, putting his face out into the wind and his hand on his heart and saying something we couldn't catch. But Rob and I both knew what he was saying into the wind, the familiar chant: *Please come back, please come back, I love you, please come back.* At the beginning of the drive, I kept turning around to say something encouraging about how I knew he could boss back his OCD bully.

"I know, I'm trying! Just one more time," he'd say, then roll down the window to do it all over again, looking partly embarrassed, partly elated, each time. Clearly, fighting the OCD bully wasn't easy. In the OCD books, the authors said fighting OCD would probably be the hardest thing a person would do in his lifetime. And to think Quinn was just a ten-year-old kid having to do this. He should have been having fun that fall, playing outside with his friends, kicking the soccer ball around, doing tricks on his bike, playing manhunt in the woods, all the things he'd done for years. I felt so helpless and distraught watching him go through this every day. Sometimes, I'd wake up in the dead of night, when the truth of how things really are never wears a mask or pretends, and I'd feel gripped by a cold fear, wondering how this had happened, wondering if Quinn would ever be himself again. On that drive to Montreal, watching him struggle, I felt a sudden fury at the goddamned OCD bully in my kid's head. I wanted to yell at it to screw off forever and leave us alone. Along the two-lane highway the leaves flashed by in a show-offy blur. A red maple was vibrating with so much scarlet that it seemed to be shimmering and I wanted to get out of the car and gape. But I couldn't because of the panic whipping through my chest that only grew when I turned around to see Quinn murmuring his secret words.

"Let's try some of those exercises," I said, trying to smile. "We'll time you to see how long you can go without having to roll down the window."

Delaying a compulsion was one of the cognitive behaviour therapy techniques I'd read about. Every second that goes by without obeying the compulsion is excruciating, but, as time passes, the anxiety gradually diminishes as the brain adapts to the feeling of not following the compulsion. Our bodies can't continually send out the fight or flight response — it's too exhausting. But of course, this is all easier said than done. All the person is thinking about is how much they *have* to obey the compulsion, and for Quinn not obeying the compulsion meant never seeing his grandpa again. There's no logic involved in OCD.

Timing Quinn between bouts of window openings seemed to be somewhat effective, but I noticed that instead of opening the window he was surreptitiously touching the handle and moving his lips. Perhaps it was a compromise with the OCD bully.

When we found the guy selling the car from his driveway, Quinn wanted to stay in the back seat of our old car rather than come with us to check out the new one. I looked at him sitting back there, staring at his running shoes. *Who are you?* I thought, *And what have you done with my real son who loves cars more than animals?*

As I made my way toward the new car, I couldn't bear turning around to watch Quinn. Now that he was alone I knew he'd be making up for having to control himself and he'd be talking away at full volume to my dad. My dad, who'd been dead for over a year now. Evidently, Quinn was still emotionally crippled by the staggering bald truth of that death, the bottomless loss. I wondered if kids actually see the reality of death for what it is. As adults we learn to shoo it away to a corner of the brain. The essential truth of our existence — nobody gets out of here alive — is one we wilfully deny. But perhaps kids, or some kids, see death for what it really is. There must be a moment when it hits all of us that our lives will one day come to a roaring halt.

It had struck my dad for the first time when he was about Quinn's age, he said, walking home from school one day. He'd actually stopped walking and just stood there for a long time, he'd often told me, because the realization that he'd die someday, and that everyone he knew would die someday, seemed too impossible, too brutally appalling, to comprehend. The only way he could come to terms with this inevitability, at least to make it more agreeable, was to think that maybe a part of a person can go on after death. He started to develop a theory that if you're always nice to people, the kindness will keep affecting others, and, in that way, you can live on after you die. This eventually led to a theory that he used to espouse on at length, boring my mother at dinner parties, that everything affects everything. He'd move a fork an inch across the table and say that that little gesture would eventually affect the people in China, spreading out from the dinner conversation to the timing of when people at the dinner had left, which, in turn, would affect the traffic of the neighbourhood, then the traffic of the city, and eventually, the lives of everyone in the world. He called it the ripple effect and it used to practically shut down my brain thinking about it. I'd imagine millions of tiny ripples all extending outward on the surface of a giant lake, ripples like halos overlapping one another, the spreading of our separate wills keeping the world afloat. Years later, I learned that my dad had been describing something that chaos theory calls the butterfly effect. As for my dad's childhood theory on kindness, he held on to that belief all his life. He was the nicest guy I ever knew.

But Quinn wasn't transforming the idea of death into anything universal. Death had hit him too hard. Instead, he was responding to death's cold hard certainty in a different way: he was shutting down.

At the wedding the next night, Quinn surprised me by dancing. He was dancing all over the floor with his cousins and aunts, jumping up and down, hugging everyone, uncharacteristically extroverted. This was a new side to him and I was partly thrilled, partly wary. When the music got too loud, his aunt Nancy suggested we go out to her car to get a bag of hand-me-down clothes for Quinn. "I want to come, too!" said Quinn. I found his enthusiasm odd since Quinn isn't especially interested in clothes, especially clothes four sizes too big for him. It had just started raining hard and the three of us ran through the parking lot toward Nancy's car. When we got the clothes and started back to the wedding hall, Quinn slipped behind us and went the other way. "What's he doing?" shouted Nancy over the deafening torrent. Through the pounding sheets of rain, I could see him alone in the corner of the parking lot, his face lit up by the street lights as he gazed up at the sky, water splashing off his bony shoulders, his hand on his heart, lips moving. I tried to get the words out to explain that Quinn was talking to my dad. Asking him to come back. I kept watching my son as the silver ropes of rain slammed the pavement and he pleaded with my dead dad to come back to us. Suddenly, I was overcome with a sense that the immediate world was made of thin glass about to shatter. The words stayed trapped at the back of my throat.

JOURNAL, EARLY OCTOBER

I'm walking along River Road tonight, trying to lose myself in the stars. When I was a kid and things were hard or confusing, I'd stare up into the never-ending maze of the night sky until my worries evaporated. "We're only one little planet," I'd say to myself. "What does any of this matter? Who cares if life is lousy down here on Earth right now? Who cares if I have a mean math teacher?"

I'm trying to do this tonight. The clear and swirling night sky, bright-banded with shimmering far-off worlds, lets me fall into it, sets my mind at ease. I have to drag Quinn out here some night, I realize. I have to tell him, Look Up! I have to make him see there's nothing to worry about when we have this streaming blaze of eternity above us. All you have to do is surrender to those stars and they'll take your worries away. When you tilt your head up into the stretches of constellations you're meandering through the centuries, the eons, the beginnings of time. And no matter where you gaze up there, you'll always find a star, a nameless solar system, unknown worlds of infinite possibility, if only our vision could reach that far. The universe goes on forever. We're as insignificant as a speck of dust. Why should we ever fret about anything with all those renegade stars wandering across the universe?

Today I visited my artist friend John to buy a little painting of his and while I was there, our friend Nathan showed up. (Even simple things that used to be fun, like talking to these two interesting and funny guys for hours, now seem weighted down by my anxiety about Quinn. You'd think these distractions might be an escape, but there is no escaping. An unwell child never leaves your mind.) Nathan, who spent twenty-seven years meditating in India, mentioned how death is such a primal fear that all the world's religions are based on the fear of death. Fear of death makes people turn to religion. No wonder people sometimes get tripped up trying to make sense of death in their own quirky way, he said.

I think about this now as I look up at the Milky Way and collapse back into my childhood cosmology. Is my dad up there somewhere, hidden in the timeless arrangement of those stars? Would telling Quinn my musings about the stars and eternity help him at all?

I will tell him, of course, but I think he might have to figure out this particular human riddle on his own.

Since visiting our family doctor in Wakefield — she'd been very understanding and concerned — we'd been entered into the Quebec health care system on an eight- to twelve-month waiting list to see someone who'd tell us whether or not we needed to see someone else who specialized in OCD, and if we did (we obviously did) we'd be put on another waiting list to see that OCD specialist.

We couldn't wait two years.

I decided we'd have to go the private route instead, which would be expensive, but it was our only option. I'd already contacted an Ottawa support group for parents with kids with OCD — and was about to attend a meeting of these parents at a diner in an Ottawa suburb — where I'd learned the names of the best private psychologists in the area who treated kids with OCD. In mid-September I'd made an appointment with a Dr. Prabhu, who kindly told me over the phone that we were doing everything right with the cognitive behaviour therapy, or actually, a branch of it known as exposure response prevention (ERP), but that unfortunately, his first available appointment wasn't until December 19. I made the appointment, or rather, grasped it like a drowning sailor on a sinking ship. I also got on the cancellation list for every other Ottawa cognitive behaviour psychologist who treated OCD.

EMAIL TO MY FRIEND DAWN IN GUELPH, EARLY OCTOBER 2013

Hi Dawn,

I'm still constantly worried about Quinn. He's still trying to get my dad to come back. It takes up most of his day. We are desperate to get help. A friend of mine here who used to live in India advised me to fly there to see an OCD specialist. We'd get an appointment right away. Is this totally crazy? I'm actually thinking about going because I don't know what else to do. We're trying the cognitive behaviour therapy stuff from the books but we still need a therapist. It's serious.

Laurie

Dear Laurie,

This is so worrisome. I'm so sorry. But don't go to India. I'm researching how you can get help in Ottawa. I'll send you some links. You're brave. So is Rob. You can get through this. Remember Quinn's birth? And how you guys got through Quinn's colic? And those years of sleep deprivation? Remember: Everything changes!

xxoo,
Dawn

CHAPTER 9

It's hard to imagine anyone being more naive about early motherhood than I was. After all my years of hitchhiking, vagabonding, and travelling to perplexing places not always on a map, I figured having a baby might be like visiting a spa: I'd lie around on a soft crush of grass under a tree while a baby slept beside me, and the baby would occasionally wake to crawl curiously around the garden, perhaps falling asleep again in a patch of sunlight.

When I brought Quinn home from the hospital I had no idea what was about to happen to my life, that I'd be so sleep deprived that I'd stagger around for a hundred days straight without more than two hours sleep in a row, that I'd be hauling him in a sleigh through the snow at midnight to get him to sleep, that (as I mentioned earlier) I'd be duct-taping his swaddled howling body to the top of the dryer to get him to stop crying. In short, I had no idea that when you tote a baby home from the hospital, life as you once knew it is effectively over.

In that first year, it seemed that every part of who I was had been stripped from me: my identity, my body, my mind, my fierce independent streak, my writing, my travelling; even my relationship had completely changed because Rob and I were now on full domestic duty instead of focusing on each other. I wanted to escape to a village of women, back to the Jamaican or Fijian villages I'd stayed in years earlier, where the large extended family of mothers, aunts, cousins, and sisters all shared in the child care. That seemed the only natural and humane way to survive being a new mother, far better than being an isolated couple trying to figure it out alone.

For the first year of Quinn's life my girlfriends would ask me, "What's it like being a mother?" Invariably, I'd reply, "I don't recommend it." When Quinn got a little older and became a sunny and fun toy-truck enthusiast who loved flying his tricycle down steep hills, I was so smitten that I couldn't recall why I'd previously said that.

But I do remember his birth. The labour came on like an ambush. I was writhing in pain on the couch at midnight, shouting, "What lousy timing! I have food poisoning!" What had I eaten that had done this to me? Surely labour wouldn't feel so *intestinal.*

The next day I was in the hospital, still writhing in pain, although now I knew it wasn't food poisoning. I recalled the day several months earlier when it hit me for the first time that I was truly pregnant, that whatever was growing inside me was going to come out. No escaping the fact. It was a singularly terrifying thought and it had stopped me cold for several seconds. And now it was happening.

I was thirty-seven when I got pregnant. I'd talked Rob into the idea. When we met each other I was thirty-five and could not believe the luck that had found me after so many years of wrong boyfriends. Before meeting him, I'd begun to think that maybe there wasn't anyone out there for me after all, that all my years of travelling had somehow marked me as someone with too many stories. Too many stories can sometimes scare men away, I'd found. I remember once going on a first date with a guy in Victoria, British Columbia, a slender artist with strawberry blond hair wisped across one brow. I'd recently escaped South Korea, where I'd gone seeking a teaching job and discovered I detested the place, had found it even more relentless than Sumatra, where I'd been just before that. But when I tried telling some of my stories to this guy in Victoria over sushi and headachy wine — there was one story, in particular, about an all-night, bone-jarring bus ride through the Sumatran jungle where I was the lone female passenger and the overhead TV played a Chinese porno — I could see his face changing as I talked, his hazel eyes flickering sideways and something tight-lipped happening around his mouth. I was scaring him away by the minute. He was still young and idealistic and even though I was only a year older, I could see he thought I was too much for him. But with Rob, here was someone who liked my stories, and who made me laugh until I couldn't get air, who played guitar and sang Tom Waits songs with a deep gravelly voice, who pretended to be an awkward insurance salesman named Howard at parties just to confuse people, who liked hiking in the woods as much as I did, who had a master's degree in forest ecology because he loved trees — trees! But what really convinced me that Rob was the right guy was the summer evening we'd walked my roommate's dog in a Guelph park. Rob was holding the leash when the dog suddenly took off after a squirrel. Instead of dropping the leash or reigning in the dog as a normal person would, Rob began running as fast as he could behind the dog so it could chase the squirrel. I stood there watching him sprint behind the dog with his arm outstretched holding the leash while the squirrel dashed for a far-off tree. I watched agog as the three of them raced through the park. Finally! This was the man I'd been waiting for. And to think I was such a world traveller and had found him in my hometown. Here was someone not only fun but funny. Also he was interesting to talk to, and kind, with Jack Kerouac rugged good looks. And he wasn't the least bit flaky. I have a low tolerance for flakiness.

But then I discovered that Rob had a problem. Soon after the dog and squirrel incident we went camping at Georgian Bay. The first evening, we were sitting in the back of his truck beside the Mediterranean-aqua bay when, to my surprise, he started playing the guitar and singing Bruce Springsteen's "Tougher Than the Rest" for me. I believe every Bruce Springsteen song has one line in it that breaks your heart a little and I was searching for that line in this song. Although Rob seemed a little reticent about discussing his feelings, he seemed to be telling me through this song that I should take a chance on him. He sang the song with so much surprising charge behind it that if the concept of being swooned no longer existed, it came back that night.

It was the second evening that the problem arose. We were walking along a gravel road beneath a thumbnail moon hanging canary-yellow in the sky and I was working up the nerve to ask him something. Finally, I took in a cool lungful of Georgian Bay air and out it came. I tried to sound casual as I asked him what he thought of the idea of having kids one day. "I don't think I want them," was his wrenching, staggeringly quick reply. I felt my heart slump and knew it wouldn't have the gumption to rise again in my chest for a long time. An excruciating silence clouded the air. Finally, he knocked the back of my hand with his and said, "Do you want kids?"

"Yes! Very much!"

"Why?"

"Why? Why? Because I loved being a kid myself!"

"That's your answer?"

My eyes slid up to the low-riding crescent moon. Clearly, I'd have to break up with him immediately.

"That's your answer?" he repeated, chuckling.

"Isn't that a good answer? If you have kids you get to relive your childhood, and be around kids all the time!" Even as I said the words I knew there was something wrong with them. I'd known from my brief early career as a primary school teacher, which, frankly, I was pretty bad at, that it doesn't work that way. Just because you like kids and liked being a kid yourself doesn't mean you'll like teaching them. In fact, liking kids makes you want to be their friend, the worst thing you can be as a teacher, or so the other teachers told me. Kids walk all over teachers like that.

"Have you been around babies?" asked Rob.

"Yeah, of course."

"Really, when?"

"Okay. So. Never."

"I guess I told you my sister had a baby when she was still living at home," he said. "The boyfriend wasn't around so my parents helped her raise the baby at our house. I was sixteen. Those weren't fun nights, all that crying, the wailing, the diapers, the tiredness I saw on my sister's face."

"But you're making it sound so unpleasant. My mother said I was an easy baby. I'm sure I'd have an easy baby, too."

"But my nephew was an easy baby. It's just that all babies are hard work. Kids are hard work."

"I'm not afraid of hard work. I've known hardship. I've taught school in the sub-Arctic. I've hitchhiked alone on several continents, hungry, lost, and friendless. I've been on Indonesian ferries in midnight, life-threatening storms. I survived junior high. How hard could a little baby be?"

I was also thinking of something else, something I couldn't name. For the past several years, when I'd substitute-taught kindergarten classes, I sometimes found myself reaching out to touch the cheek of a little kid when he or she came to my desk. I couldn't help it. I was overwhelmed with how impossibly soft their cheeks were. It filled me with a kind of deep sweet longing, a secret hope that someday I'd have my own child with soft cheeks to stroke. And at those same desks I'd sometimes seen photos of the young teachers whose class I was taking, photos of her with her husband and baby, all of them beaming at the Sears photographer in front of the mottled background. The husbands didn't look terribly interesting or handsome, probably watched a lot of TV sports, but still. Still. They were smiling radiantly and holding a baby with soft cheeks. I wanted to be in one of those pictures one day.

And now that dream was slipping away from me. The man I wanted to spend my life with was saying he wasn't interested in having kids. The only reason I didn't break up with Rob the next week was because he said he was open to my talking him into the idea.

So for the next couple of months, that's what I did. I talked him into the idea of me, him, and a baby. I'm not even sure what I said exactly since it was true that I was ignorant of every aspect of the realities of having a child. I wasn't an aunt and all my girlfriends were, so far, childless. My only girl-friend who had kids had moved to Atlanta. I remember telling Rob that I'd have to know his decision soon, one way or the other. If he wasn't interested in having kids I'd have to find someone who was. Time was running out for me. He told me he needed another week to think about it, then went on a solo canoe trip to Algonquin Park. When he came back he suggested we go for a walk. We went to the same park where he'd let the dog chase the squirrel. My heart was ricocheting callously around my ribcage as we walked beside the river under a grove of tall maples. I was expecting the worst.

Finally, he said, a little nervously, "So … I've decided."

"And?" I took a deep breath. "No, wait!" I inhaled deeply, imagining float-ing down the river in a rowboat by myself. Maybe I could adopt a child from another country, spend my life travelling in far-off Eastern lands with that child. Everything would be fine. Oh, God. This was hell. "Okay, you can tell me now."

He cleared his throat. "I want to go ahead. To do it all. Get married, have a kid. I want that. I do."

The trees around us began to blur in my vision. I stared at Rob for a long time. The moment shook me in its unexpectedness, like a shooting star searing by from another galaxy.

"Really? You do?" I jumped up in the air, high. He laughed and we hugged each other. I was going to be in one of those Sears photographs. One day, we were going to have a baby.

And now, three years later, that baby felt like a burning bowling ball ripping through my intestines. The labour wasn't going well. In fact, nothing about this birth was going as I'd imagined. I'd imagined that having a baby would come close to what my touchy-feely baby books had promised: a natural birth in which labour pains could be blissful. What a crock.

I kept thinking, hasn't evolution had time to work on this? Must women really endure this much pain after all these millennia? Evolution wasn't keeping up. And you'd think anyone who'd been through this once would surely never do it again. Not only that, they'd tell their cave women friends never to do it. As soon as our species began communicating verbally you'd think that would have been the end of it. Even nonverbal communication could have conveyed the idea simply enough. A simple finger swiping across the neck to indicate BIRTH = BAD IDEA. Don't even think about it!

Aside from the pain of contractions, there was the matter of where the baby was being born. We'd planned on having our baby at a lovely little birthing centre not far from Wakefield. The baby would enter the world gently, into the loving arms of two midwives in a candlelit room on a cozy bed, or possibly, in a tub of warm water. Music of our choice could be played in the background, and wholesome vegetarian meals would be served. No drugs to ease the pain would be allowed, but that was okay since pain was just a state of mind. It had all sounded like some sort of love-in, a celestial, exotic event that we could cherish for years, and, perhaps, digitally record.

But we weren't at the lovely birthing centre. We were in a French hospital in Ottawa because of a law stating that if a woman's water breaks and she hasn't begun dilating within twenty-four hours, she must deliver in a hospital rather than with a midwife. That's why I'd spent the day in a dingy-walled hospital room on a hard bed, wired to monitors, with a steady stream of nurses going on and off their hectic shifts. I'd also been induced with oxytocin. When you're induced, your contractions come on much stronger than ordinary contractions, like wild horses thundering across your kidneys. The obstetrician came in early on to tell me I should have an epidural, which I refused, and then I didn't see him again for hours. Finally, at midnight, after twenty-four hours of more pain than I knew was humanly possible, I recall shouting, "Give me the epidural!"

After the epidural kicked in, the contractions were just something to watch on a monitor. But then the monitor started showing that the baby's heart was slowing down dangerously because of the oxytocin. By this time it was 2:00 a.m. and there was just one night nurse left on duty in the short-staffed ward — it was almost Christmas. Every time the monitor started beeping to indicate red alert, the sprite little nurse, named Josie, would run in frantically to tell me the baby's heart was slowing down, then she'd stick her fingers inside me to tickle the baby's head to revive him until the monitor showed his heart charging up again. Every time this happened, I'd look at Rob, terrified. I simply could not comprehend that all this time there'd been a catastrophe concealed in this pregnancy. I hadn't seen it coming: a baby with a fragile heart. I have no idea how many times Josie saved our baby's life by tickling his tiny head. I'd never heard of saving a life by tickling but I was so grateful to Josie that I contemplated naming our baby son after her. Come on, baby, I was thinking, don't die, you're being tickled! See how fun life will be? One of those times when Josie was trying to revive the baby, she started yelling for another nurse to come help her. No other nurse appeared — the ward was hauntingly empty — so she got Rob to help by manoeuvring my body around to kick-start the baby's heart. All the while she kept yelling for the no-show nurse to come help.

In that grey, morgue-like room, it was just me, Rob, Josie, and an unborn baby with a dead-beat heart.

Finally, the doctor rushed in to tell me I should have an emergency C-section. My own heart sank. This was not what I'd imagined. Half an hour later, I was wheeled down the hall into a fluorescent-lit surgery room. The lights were blinding. My baby will leave the womb and enter Las Vegas, I kept thinking. My arms were shackled down crucifix-style at my wrists, Rob was above me, dressed in green, sterile scrubs, wearing a mask. Everything was happening at lightning speed. Suddenly, I was sliced open, but all I could see was the doctor's face as he reached inside me. For a moment, he looked puzzled. "The baby's backward," he said. "And the cord is around his neck." Jeepers, I thought, this baby has *issues*. Then the doctor got the other doctors to count to four. They counted, pushed down on me, then, suddenly, miraculously, the room was filled with the sound of a baby crying. A baby crying, I thought. There really *was* a baby in there all along. Imagine that!

And suddenly it didn't matter so much about the inhospitability of the operating room. The marvel of a baby emerging into the world overwhelmed the blinding lights, the cold, hard medical equipment, and the surgical masks. As I waited to see my son, I felt transported, weightless, full of the wonder of human beauty that must come with all births, as if some ancient part of my mind were stirring in recognition. They only let me see him for a moment. Since my arms were fettered down all I could do was kiss his cheek — a child's cheek of my own to kiss! Rob was beside me, clearly overtaken, able only to say, "Wow!" several dozen times. Then they scurried our baby off somewhere with Rob following, saying he wouldn't let him out of his sight. I was whizzed off to a recovery room, wanting desperately to be with my baby but also so dazed from the drugs and so exhausted from not having slept in so long that my mind wasn't actually working. I think an hour or so passed before someone floated me down a long white hall on a gurney until we arrived at a closed door. Then that door opened. I had no stomach muscles left to sit up, but I could turn my head to see that inside the quiet, darkened room, Rob was in a chair in the corner holding Quinn in a blanket.

There are certain moments one remembers all one's life and those moments are burned into the heart — the fragile, resilient, joyful heart — and later, years down the road, those moments can take your breath away, take up your whole life, or perhaps, save your life. That was one of those moments.

CHAPTER 10

Hi Tina,

Quinn's OCD is getting worse all the time. Yesterday he came home from school and said he couldn't do any of his work because he told himself he had to erase and cross out everything he'd written. I took a look and saw that he'd scrawled sentences across the bottom of the page of his notebook, sentences that were all crossed out or erased. This meant that he didn't get any of his schoolwork done and the next day, had to stay in for recess to do the work he'd missed. When he came home he said, "My life is a complete misery because of this fucking OCD and I wish I was dead!" Then he burst out crying and threw his bag across the room. Can you believe it? Quinn, the most undramatic child who ever lived. I immediately made an emergency call to the Quebec medical people (the people who put us on the two-year waiting list). I only got their voice mail. I was almost hysterical when I left the message, my heart bashing a hole in my chest. I said, "Someone has to see my son. We can't wait two years. My child just told me he wished he was dead. We need help now! Please!"

They didn't even call back.

I never thought life would be like this. I guess that's what people always say when their world is falling apart.

So long for now.

Laurie

In the midst of Quinn's early days of unravelling, I still had to finish teaching some English as a second language classes in Wakefield, and have a tooth extracted (something that normally might have caused mild alarm but under the circumstances barely registered), and I was supposed to hold a writing workshop at my house one Saturday. I'd scheduled it months earlier and couldn't cancel. On top of this, the day after my workshop I'd be driving to Montreal to teach for two days at a college there. Rob was also busy then but, luckily, Rob's sister volunteered to take Quinn for a night. As usual Quinn was excited about visiting his aunt. But when she tried taking him to her curling club, he was afraid to get out of her car. A couple of days later, I Skyped Rob from Tina's apartment in Montreal. Rob looked as if he'd been through a natural disaster: he was pale and visibly shaken. Quinn said hi to me, mumbled he'd be right back, then disappeared. I wondered why he wasn't at school.

"Things aren't good," said Rob, when Quinn had left and then he told me why he'd kept him home. "We're going through these cognitive behaviour OCD workbooks and we've made an Excel chart, to list all his behaviours so he can rate them one to five. It's like a Richter scale of anxiety. The 'ones' are supposed to be the stuff that doesn't cause much anxiety. Those are the things he's supposed to work on not doing first, the easiest things. But he's rated every single behaviour as a five. That means not doing those things causes the highest possible anxiety. Like a full-blown panic attack. If I leave him alone for a minute, it's an OCD-fest. When I had a shower this morning I knew what he was doing in his room."

"What?" I choked out.

"Climbing up on his dresser to reach that picture on the wall." I knew what picture he meant. It was of Quinn as a baby surrounded by his grandparents, all of them smiling under some trees on a summer evening by the Ottawa River. "He's touching your dad in the photo. Asking him to come back. The usual. It's not enough just to say the words any more. Now he has to touch an image of your dad at the same time."

"Jesus."

"That's probably what he's doing right now." Rob stopped talking. Across the invisible miles between us, all we could do was stare helplessly into the abyss of each other.

I felt a rising panic in my chest. *How could this be happening to our family? How could there have been a crisis hidden inside our happiness?* I inhaled a long ragged breath. Just then, Halla hurtled into the apartment, and for the first time I felt something like envy at how normal and carefree other people's kids seemed. Quinn used to be like this, and not so long ago, either. Halla was thrilled I was Skyping with his friend. "Is Quinn there, too? Can I talk to him?" His brown eyes were wide with innocent anticipation.

"That's a great idea, Halla."

Watching the two boys talk — mostly about Minecraft and an upcoming cross-country race that Quinn would be running in — the envy I'd felt earlier was swept away by a deep thankfulness for their friendship. Quinn seemed almost his old self talking to Halla. If you have OCD and are immersed in something else, like an interesting conversation or playing with a friend, you can temporarily suspend your OCD. This seemed to be happening as the boys talked. I was even more glad now that I'd be driving Tina and Halla, who was homeschooled, back with me to Wakefield that day. Thanksgiving was coming up and we'd all be spending several days together. Even my mother was coming.

CHAPTER 11

When Tina, Halla, and I arrived that evening, Quinn met us at the front door, his eyes shining with his news, or in my mind, with his latest obsession: he was going to win the two-kilometre cross-country race that Friday. It was all he could talk about. The cross-country race was an annual event involving all the schools in the district and it was held at the Wakefield School because it bordered a hilly forest full of trails. Quinn's obsession was still tied to his grandpa. If he won the race, his grandpa would come back. If he didn't win, he wouldn't come back. If he tapped the photo on the wall, closed his eyes, and said, "Come back" ten times, he'd win the race. Or perhaps he'd have to tap it twenty times, or thirty times, depending on the time of day. The photo of my dad also had to be the last thing he'd look at before going to sleep at night and the first thing he'd open his eyes to in the morning. He'd also taken to climbing a pine tree at the end of our laneway every evening exactly at sunset to ask my dad to come back. Keeping up with the various rituals wasn't easy for us. They were a moving target. OCD was a shape-shifter. We also realized that the compulsions we saw were just the tip of a deep uncharted iceberg. The mental compulsions inside his head were even worse, plaguing Quinn, and keeping him from sleeping at night. He was beginning to have dark circles under his eyes.

One night before the race, Quinn and I sat down together on the couch to go through some of the exercises in the OCD workbook. In the background, the host of a CBC radio show, a former musician, was talking about

Neil Young. I flipped through the OCD book. One exercise asked the child to draw a picture of himself fighting off the OCD monster.

"I can't draw it," said Quinn. "It's too hard."

"But you love drawing. You're such a good artist." I thought of the stacks of sketchbooks he'd gone through in his life, replicating cars, bicycles, forests, and cities.

"I'd just have to erase it if I drew it. I have to erase everything. That's why I walk back the same way I came. To erase that I was here. To get everything back to zero."

"Well, what would you draw in the workbook if you could? What would a picture of you fighting the OCD monster look like?" Neil Young was singing "Sugar Mountain" on the radio and the song drifted into a rusty place inside me where I hadn't been for a long time. Quinn seemed to be contemplating, staring hard at the OCD book.

"I know!" Quinn's face lit up. "I'd draw Grandpa and me running the race together, holding hands, being chased by the OCD monster. Then winning the race!"

Somehow I didn't think that's what the authors of the book were going for.

"I hope to God he loses that race," said Rob to Tina and me later that night when we were sitting around a fire outside and the kids had gone to bed. "Winning would be the worst thing for him. Winning would show him his superstitions are valid, that the OCD bully has control, that all those compulsions paid off. We have to keep telling him that his need to win is the OCD, not him, and he should just enjoy the race."

"Thank goodness for Owen," I said. Owen was a boy in Quinn's class who always came first in the cross-country race. Quinn always came second. It happened every year.

On the morning of the race, the air was crisp, the sky a deep sapphire blue that you only see in autumn, and maple trees were clutching the last of summer's green in their arms. I was at the school to volunteer as a spotter for the runners, to watch in case a kid slipped in the mud, tripped on a root, or sprained an ankle trudging up and down the steep wooded inclines of the forest. But mainly, I was there to see Quinn.

As I walked through the schoolyard toward my assigned spot up in the woods, I was suddenly struck with a hollow feeling as I passed by kids Quinn had known for years, playing soccer and basketball, laughing, running, living their gloriously unfractured lives. It was hard to accept that fate could be so unfair, that the lives of these other kids seemed so unscarred. Then I immediately felt selfish, thinking of starving children in war-torn countries, or kids who'd died or had some fatal disease. Just thinking of that kind of suffering and the parents of those children made my heart unexpectedly swell with an overwhelming empathy, which hit me harder than it ever had before.

I ran into my friend Anna as I walked toward the woods. Anna, who was from England, was one of the most caring people I'd ever met. She was a psychotherapist with a lilting Yorkshire accent and auburn ringlets. When she had first moved to Canada she used to look after Quinn sometimes when he was a baby. She'd always loved Quinn.

"Laurie, I have something to tell you." Her eyebrows were knitted with concern. She put her hand on my arm. I braced myself. "I saw Quinn yesterday walking his bike up the hill to school. He was … stuck."

"Stuck?" My ribcage suddenly felt like a corset.

"He was just standing there with his bike, not moving. Frozen. For a long time. I asked him if he needed help and he started crying. I asked him what was wrong and he said he didn't want to go to school. We talked for a bit, then he seemed to gather up the strength to keep going up the hill to school."

I tried not to cry myself as I felt my throat clenching but it was no use. So this was why he'd been taking so long to get home from school. He was getting stuck. Was he trying to stop time? What was this particular OCD ritual about? My eyes felt the stabbing pressure of tears. This was all too much. I couldn't speak. Anna hugged me and told me she'd help us, that she'd do everything she could, call all her contacts in her therapy world, help us figure it out. We weren't alone. Quinn is strong, she kept saying. He'll get through this. He has strong parents who love him more than anything. I nodded, tried to smile, and felt the hard knot in my chest loosening. Through my tears I stared down at the yellow leaves lying belly-up on the ground, dried and pointy like claws. I still couldn't speak but knew Anna would understand.

An hour or so later the gun went off for Quinn's race. Up until then, I'd been standing at the top of the first big hill with another volunteer mother as packs of kids surged by us every fifteen minutes. Between bouts of stampeding kids — some running fast, some running at a jogger's pace, some barely running at all — the other mother was promoting the virtues of her paleo diet. I didn't have it in me to question her. What did it matter? When she stopped talking midsentence, I followed her gaze. On the trail through the trees, Quinn and Owen were charging like rams up the steep hill, panting hard, leaving a throng of other ten-year-old boys in their wake. While they ran off toward the cemetery, I sprinted down the other way to the finish line, musty leaves crackling beneath my feet as I crunched over them. Rob was at the finish line, too. I wondered if his heart was thundering like mine was. It was an odd feeling *not* to want your kid to win a race, especially when your kid was so set on it. I had to remind myself it was the OCD bully demanding he win, not Quinn.

At the finish line, we watched for the runners to emerge out of the woods. I wondered if some of the boys from other schools might have overtaken Owen and Quinn. It was possible they'd spent all their energy too early. But suddenly, there they were, Owen and Quinn storming out of the woods, and running neck and neck with fifty metres to go. The schoolyard felt electric as kids roared and cheered, jumping up and down, shouting their names. Time seemed to slow down for me as I watched Quinn, a startling blaze of velocity dashing over the Earth. Was he thinking of outrunning Death at that moment, beating it at its own game? Or was he just Quinn, my little boy who'd always loved to run? I felt a sudden twinge of aching nostalgia for his rolly-legged toddler self so determined to run as fast and far as possible before tumbling to the ground.

Then it happened: Owen shot across the finish line first. A second later, Quinn crossed it.

It was over. Like every other year, Quinn had come in second. I exhaled deeply. Things seemed restored to their normal order.

"Way to go, Quinn!" Rob and I shouted.

Owen and Quinn were bent over, hands on their knees, trying to catch their breaths. Their friends surrounded them, patting them on their backs. A first and second place would give the school lots of points in the overall competition.

When the other kids cleared away, I went over to Quinn to give him a hug. His body was hot, his face flushed. A big smile broke across his face as he looked at me. "Did you see how close I came, Mummy? Usually I'm like, two car lengths behind Owen. This time I was right there behind him. I could have touched him!"

"You were so fast! You ran so hard! I'm so proud of you!" Rob took a photo as Quinn and I grinned for the camera.

For a few glorious moments, we were all free of the OCD bully.

But when Quinn stood on the podium an hour later — all the kids who'd competed and a bunch of parents and teachers were watching — I couldn't help noticing his movements were jerky. I saw his lips moving when they put the medal around his neck and I knew that he was talking to my dad. I wondered what he was saying, what new bargain he was trying to strike to bring him back. Later, when I went looking for him in the school to give him money for pizza, I spotted him in the hallway jumping across the patterns of linoleum tiles. His hand was on his heart and he was murmuring. My own heart plummeted at how fractured and off-kilter everything was again.

I didn't know it at the time but perhaps felt it lurking somewhere: The day of the race would be the last day he'd attend school for almost a month.

CHAPTER 12

My mother arrived by train that afternoon. Tina, Halla, Quinn, and I picked her up at the Ottawa train station. While Tina and I waited in the car for the boys to find my mother inside, we watched flocks of visitors arriving for Thanksgiving weekend, while, overhead, flocks of Canada geese headed south. Every day now we'd see the geese, coming from the far north, beating across the sky in dark waves as they honked their way to Florida. I felt like joining them. When Tina and I finally saw my mother emerging from the station, we chuckled darkly about the fact that it was social Halla chatting away with my mother, whom he had never met, while Quinn quietly pulled her suitcase behind them.

That night, while Halla was brushing his teeth, I looked in on Quinn in his bedroom. He was kneeling on his dresser and reaching up to touch the picture of my dad, mumbling to himself with his eyes closed, chanting the same phrase over and over about coming back. I cleared my throat. "Quinn, sweetie, that's enough. Don't let the OCD bully make you do this."

He opened his eyes, shouted, "Go away!" and looked at me with what I can only describe as hatred. The look shot a voltage of dread through me. I'd never seen that look on my son before. How had he become so unmoored from his old life? How could I return him to being the boy he really was, the boy who looked at me with a smile or a giggle on his face? Quinn's giggle used to be so infectious that a friend of ours had actually recorded two-year-old Quinn giggling so she could remember what happiness sounded like. Where had that boy gone?

Later that night, Rob said something about how the real Quinn was deep inside, struggling to get out. "He hates doing this stuff but he can't not do it. The real Quinn we know wouldn't do any of it. We can't take any of it personally." I knew Rob was right — Rob was so much better at being patient and rational and level-headed in all this than I was — but it didn't mean I didn't feel like buckling in half and sobbing at losing my son before my eyes.

The next morning my mother just happened to pass Quinn's bedroom and saw him up on the dresser, touching the picture and beseeching her dead husband to come back. It's one thing to hear how dire a situation is on the phone from your daughter, but to witness something so unfathomable and deeply disturbing about your own grandson with your own eyes torpedoes everything to the surface. I stood in the hallway with a view of my tiny mother staring up at Quinn on the dresser, and a view of Tina and Halla on the couch in the living room. On seeing Quinn, my mother shot me a desperate look, like someone who suddenly finds herself utterly lost, then she turned back to him. Tina, Halla, and I listened, frozen in place, as my mother's words began to fill the house.

"Oh, Quinn my love, Grandpa's not coming back. Touching that picture won't do anything. Grandpa is dead. People die. That's what happens. People have been waiting two thousand years for Jesus to come back but it's not going to happen. Grandpa wouldn't want you to ask him to come back. He wouldn't want you to be sad. He'd want you to be your old self again. I miss Grandpa, too. I miss him so much that I dream about him every night and I miss him every minute. I understand why you want him back. I'd like him to come back, too. But he's not going to." She stopped talking as a long single note of a high-pitched wail of sorrow began to drift out of the room. For a second I didn't even realize it was coming from Quinn, so unearthly it sounded. My mother continued, her voice remaining firm. "But Quinn, *I'm* still alive. I'm right here and I'm your grandma and I love you more than anyone in the world. I've loved you since I first held you when you were two days old. I'm alive and I love you."

Just as her words had filled the house, now silence rushed into every dusty corner and up to the highest ceiling beams.

It felt like a giant pause button had been pushed. Nobody moved. But then, to my surprise, Quinn got down from the dresser, forgoing the rest of the please come back ritual, and threw himself into my mother's arms. They hugged a long time while Quinn sobbed. Tina mouthed, "Oh, my God, oh, my God!" from the couch, giving me the thumbs-up. I couldn't speak. I was too overcome with admiration for my strong and wise mother, and the scene unfolding in front of me.

Of course, I thought, it had always been my mother who had loved Quinn, her only grandchild, so wholeheartedly, playing and reading with him, buying him books, making him healthy meals, worrying about his every cold, wondering about the comings and goings of his days. Although my dad loved Quinn, it was my mother who'd stayed with us the first six weeks of Quinn's life, who'd spent so many hours down on the floor playing with him as a toddler, searching the stores for some Thomas the Tank Engine water tower or little elfin dolls to drive his toy cars. Sometimes when the three of us were visiting my parents in Guelph, she'd sing out before dinner, *Wash your hands!* and Quinn and I would race to the bathroom sink, giggling, nudging each other out of the way, and I'd have the uncanny feeling that Quinn was my little brother rather than my son, and she was our mother, so much more motherly than I was.

Why hadn't I said this to Quinn more often? *Grandma is still alive.*

For the next four hours after the talk on the dresser, Quinn didn't display a single OCD behaviour. This was the longest he'd gone without doing anything OCDish in weeks. It was as if he'd snapped out of it. Later in the morning, when the boys were playing outside, Halla came in for a glass of water. My mother and I were in the kitchen — she jokingly saying, "I better darn-well stay alive now as long as I can" — when Halla came over and touched her sleeve. "I wanted to tell you that what you said to Quinn did wonders for him. We've been playing out there and I haven't seen him do any OCD all morning." An enormous smile took over my mother's face as she put her hand on Halla's slim shoulder and told him how lucky Quinn was to have a friend like him.

Later, I came to realize that my mother's speech to Quinn on his dresser that morning had been one of a few incidents where a window had opened, however briefly, and for a while, Quinn stopped using the protection of OCD to mask his pain. Her words somehow broke through his shell and must have reached his very core, thus that haunting wailing sound. For a brief while he'd let the truth come inside.

But like a drunken neighbour at a barbeque who finally leaves but annoyingly returns after dark, Quinn's OCD gradually made its unwelcome reappearance over the course of the day. That night, Quinn actually took the framed photo of my dad off the wall and stuck it under his pillow. When I wanted to read the boys a chapter of *The Time Thief*, Halla on the bottom bunk and Quinn and me on the top, Quinn couldn't make space for me because he said he had to stay in the exact position he landed in when he'd jumped into bed. He was sprawled diagonally on his back with his bent arm elbowing upward, one foot raised high in the air, knee slightly bent, staring straight up at the ceiling.

"That's ridiculous," I heard myself say in exasperation to his comically frozen form. "You're actually giving up hearing what happens next in the book to do that? Are you planning on sleeping with your elbow and foot in the air?"

Halla popped out of his bed to take a look. "Whoa, that's so not what I was expecting," he said. At this point, Quinn broke out laughing, which made Halla and me laugh, too. Quinn must have realized how silly this whole thing was. He didn't move from his position, though. It seemed that every so often, he'd realize how ludicrous and funny his OCD was, but it was rarely ludicrous and funny enough to stop doing it.

This meant I couldn't read the boys the book. We weren't supposed to enable the OCD. Enabling the OCD bully shows the child that the bully has power over us. "Your OCD bully isn't the boss of me," we were always saying. I had to tell him that since he wasn't making room for me, I couldn't read the story that night. When I turned off the bedroom light, the last things I saw were Quinn's elbow and foot still wavering above his body, like spare parts that didn't know where they belonged.

The next day I was on the phone with my sister in Colorado. I'd emailed her about how serious Quinn's condition was and now she was determined to find a solution over the phone. "Would a couple of days at Disney World help? I could take him there. Nobody could be unhappy at Disney World." When I dissuaded her from that suggestion she said his problem must stem from seasonal affective disorder and the grey skies of Canada. "He's just depressed," she said. "The sun never comes out where you live."

"First of all, that's so not true," I said. "If you'd said this to me in February, when the sun really doesn't come out much, I'd have thought grey skies could be a contributing factor. But summer just ended and the sun has been out for months on end. His vitamin D count is fine. It's OCD. It's not the weather."

"Still, I think Disney World would help. And more omega-3." At this point I gave the phone to my mother, who suggested to my sister something more helpful than Disney World, such as some money to help pay for the child psychologist bills. My sister and her wealthy husband sent us money straight away.

We took my mother to see Quinn's first indoor soccer game of the season, wondering if the OCD bully would interfere with his playing. From a bench on the sidelines we watched Quinn perform various dekes around other players and saw him running at lightning speed up the field on some breakaways. Nobody there could have known how tormented his mind was. It seemed the thrill and immediacy of soccer was the perfect antidote to OCD. The OCD bully didn't stand a chance during the adrenaline-pumping moments when Quinn was close to the ball. Only when there wasn't much action on the field did we see Quinn struggling, jerking his body, walking backward, hopping on one foot, or putting his hand on his heart and murmuring up at the ceiling rafters. At one point, we could see him across the field on the bench beside some teammates waiting their turn to go back on. When one of the coaches, a French-speaking woman built like a refrigerator, called for him to go back out, Quinn didn't move. He was immobilized on the bench. We watched her go over to him, grab his arm, and physically yank him up. In seconds he was back on the field and even shot us a smile. "Well that worked," said Rob, chuckling. "The yank. Let's try it at home." Later in the game, when Quinn made a beautiful pass to a player who scored, my mother turned to me with tears in her eyes. "Your dad would have loved to have seen this." I blinked back tears. She was right. My sports-loving dad would have been so proud and thrilled to watch Quinn play soccer.

EMAIL, OCTOBER 14, 2013

Hi Tina,

Since you and Halla left yesterday, Quinn is going in and out of these strange trances in which he seems totally lost. Somehow, my mum is able to bring him back out of it by talking to him. But now I'm worried that after she leaves tomorrow I won't be able to do it myself. He keeps touching her arm, an OCD thing, probably because he associates her with my dad. I'm sure he's thinking he can magically communicate with my dad through her.

Anyway, I'm feeling a bit better about it all right now because I just spent the last hour (jeez, it's almost midnight!) doing an experiment. I tried hypnotizing Quinn to get him to stop worrying and get to sleep. (I've made an appointment for him with a hypnotherapist and thought I'd give it a try myself.) Before starting this tonight, Quinn had been OCDing like crazy as he lay next to me, totally lost in another world. I got him to take a bunch of deep breaths and then I began this long rambling story in a slow monotone voice. I was making it up as I went along. It went something like this:

"You're totally relaxed. You're standing on a white sand beach with the ocean waves lapping at your feet. The sun feels warm on your skin. A little breeze is ruffling your hair. Nobody is around. It's just you, alone on this long white-sand, powdery beach. You start walking along the shore. You're so happy and free. No worries in the world. You start running a little. It feels so good to run that you just keep running down the beach, happy and free." I yammered on like that for at least twenty minutes. Amazingly, Quinn seemed to be relaxing, not flinching or doing any OCD at all. I couldn't believe it was actually working and he was getting a break from OCD. Then I said, "You see someone far ahead on the beach. You keep running. When you get closer you see the person is Grandpa. He says, Hi Quinn! You give him a hug and the two of you run along together. Happy and free. Then Grandpa says he's a little tired and he'd like to sit and rest on this beautiful beach and you should go on and keep running. Happy and free. You give him a hug goodbye and keep running. You feel so happy and free. You've let Grandpa go and you know he's happy back there, sitting on the beach. You're back to running and feel so happy and free. Happy and free. Happy and free...."

Quinn was breathing so deeply and seemed so relaxed that I thought he was asleep. Just as I was leaving, he whispered, Don't leave yet, just sing "Moon River" first. So I sang the song twice and he lay there smiling peacefully. If only this were the end of it. If only a simple old song that I used to sing him as a toddler was all that was needed to free him from his torment. I could hear his breathing changing toward the end and realized he was asleep. My experiment actually seemed to work. Fingers crossed about how he'll be tomorrow.

xxoo
Laurie

I continued my email the next morning.

Tina, he's back to OCD-ville. But at least the experiment put him to sleep. He asked me if I'll do it again tonight.

CHAPTER 13

Afer my mother left and Thanksgiving weekend was over, it was obvious that Quinn was in no condition to go to school. He was engaging in a storm of compulsions and hourly changing rituals of magical thinking that debilitated his entire day. Going to school was out of the question. He couldn't even read anymore because he had to read the sentences backward after reading them the first time, to erase them. Rob proposed he and Quinn spend the mornings doing the exposure response prevention exercises they'd been working on.

At the end of the school day, I went to talk to Quinn's teacher Mr. DeFranco, to pick up school work Quinn could possibly do at home and to explain why he was absent. The young teacher's eyes were full of concern as I spoke. "Come over here," he said, beckoning me to Quinn's desk. He pulled out Quinn's math workbook. "I was going to tell you this so I'm glad you're here now. Take a look." I stared down at the pages of the workbook, which was supposed to be full of solved multiplication problems. Instead of numbers, tiny words were scrawled in Quinn's printing all across the bottom of the pages, the same words, dozens of times over, the same ones we'd heard for weeks: "Please come back, please come back. I love you. Please come back." I flipped back the pages. It was the same plea over and over, a boy's impossible prayer hidden in a worn math notebook.

I felt the room starting to spin. A kid I knew, a casual friend of Quinn's, bounded into the class just then to riffle through his desk to find something. Quinn had helped teach this kid how to ride a unicycle not that long ago.

The boy said hi to me and his teacher and shot out of the room again: untroubled, shoes untied, a regular kid on his way to build a fort or buy a chocolate bar with his friends at the *dépanneur*. Why wasn't that Quinn? I felt the cruel randomness of life weighing me down like never before.

It was around this time, in mid-October when Quinn wasn't at school, that I could feel myself withdrawing from my familiar social world. It didn't matter that I knew people's lives were never perfect and that life could be complicated for everyone. The people around me still gave off the impression that things were fine, but the happy family life that Rob and Quinn and I had known had long ago skipped town.

Rob told me that night how hard it had been for him to find behaviours for Quinn to work on, meaning behaviours Quinn wasn't supposed to engage in, or at least behaviours that he was supposed to try delaying for a period of time. The idea of ERP, the so-called "gold standard" for treating OCD, is to expose yourself to your fears by not performing any of the reassuring compulsions brought on by the fears. You place yourself in a situation deliberately designed to exacerbate your anxiety. In other words, you force yourself to endure the constant temptation to revert to your defensive rituals. You hang yourself out there, often in something close to terror, waiting for the misery to subside. A child who has a fear of germs, a common type of OCD, makes herself touch a doorknob that she believes is covered with deadly germs. After touching the doorknob for a set amount of time, the anxiety level decreases and the child realizes that nothing catastrophic has happened. She is habituating herself to the anxiety. Just as neurologists have shown that every time you resist acting on your anger, you're actually rewiring your brain to be calmer, so with exposing yourself to your anxiety are you rewiring your brain, forming new cognitive pathways. The next time, the child can try touching the doorknob longer. Eventually, the compulsion loses its appeal. The more one is able to avoid acting on the compulsion, the weaker the bad connection becomes. You're recircuiting your brain. If someone has a compulsion to put things in order, he might expose himself to clutter for a few minutes without touching anything. It's facing the thing you fear a little at a time until you've finally conquered it. The longer you've had OCD the longer this therapy takes since well-worn cognitive pathways have deep grooves and take time to be remapped in your brain. This is why the sooner you start ERP the better.

Rob could relate to all this, and to Quinn's anxiety, much more than I could, since Rob himself — the most laid-back, easy-going person I knew — had something called generalized anxiety disorder (meaning Quinn had inherited some pretty interesting genes, the sidewalk-crack-stepping kind of OCD from his mother, and hidden anxiety from his dad). Rob's fear was being trapped in small spaces. (Interestingly, the most common phobias are of primal dangers, such as snakes, spiders, heights, and small closed spaces, rather than of more realistic modern ones, like car accidents.) Rob knew his fear wasn't logical and that's how he could relate to Quinn's OCD. He learned that to overcome his fear, he should make himself sleep in a tent in our living room, or make himself sit in the back seat of a car — situations that even thinking about could sometimes cause near panic attacks — but he found if he exposed himself to these things, he could ride out the waves of anxiety. Exposure worked.

Quinn's obsession was a bit trickier since it wasn't concrete. Rob tried to get him to say aloud, "Grandpa isn't coming back," but even hearing Rob suggest this sent Quinn racing into his room to climb up on the dresser and touch the picture, to loudly declare the opposite, as if this were the Middle Ages and Rob had uttered some kind of blasphemy that needed rectifying.

This made me think about how far back magical thinking goes in human evolution, back to when our primitive minds were so fraught with fear that we engaged in spells, curses, witchcraft, and superstition to ward off evil or to make things happen or to try to control things we had no control over. And magical thinking isn't a phenomenon confined exclusively to the remote past. Today's religions are full of magical thinking and superstition. In fact, for some reason that still isn't understood, religious rituals weirdly echo OCD rituals. I was reminded of this every time Quinn placed his hand on his heart, looked up at the sky, and started in on his chant. Where did he get this? Certainly not from his upbringing. It made me think of Catholics making the sign of the cross over their hearts and saying Hail Marys while counting rosary beads, all in the hopes of making something happen, or warding some evil away. Hyperreligiosity, or scrupulosity, is a major feature of OCD. Five centuries ago, Ignatius of Loyola described the condition of scrupulosity as being overly anxious and obsessed with doing religious rituals perfectly. Other religious rituals besides the Catholic ones that mysteriously mimic OCD rituals include numerology and counting, repetition of mantras, hours of body cleansing, and rules about how to enter and leave holy places. Orthodox Hindu Brahmins can spend six hours a day in body cleansing rituals. They also have rules dictating the repetition of magic numbers, which foot to put down first when getting out of bed, and how to enter and leave the temple. Orthodox Jews engage in highly complex ritualistic eating and cleansing rituals, have strict rules about entering and leaving holy places, and also recite special numbers. Muslims must enter and leave mosques and cleanse their bodies in very specific ways. The list of striking similarities between religious rituals and the rituals of OCD sufferers goes on. Not performing these rituals leaves both the religious participant and the OCD sufferer with a sense of dread. And if these religious rituals aren't performed "correctly" the person makes himself do them all over again. Where do these religious rituals come from and why do people with OCD — even little kids who know nothing of religion — also perform them? Nobody seems to know.

I wondered if magical thinking was genetically encoded in the primitive part of our brain — *patternicity* at work — and whether people with OCD were accessing those primitive vestiges. Certainly, for some reason, those primitive vestiges were inexplicably emerging. Was some long-forgotten corner of the ancestral brain being provoked? I thought about how ubiquitous magical thinking is across cultures. I recalled how Fiji and Southeast Asia had been full of superstition. Even in Canada, kids come up with magical thinking all the time on their own. I remember when I was a child my friend told me that if you drove past a graveyard and didn't lift your feet off the car floor you lost five percent of your sex appeal. I lifted my feet off the car floor for years after that. I didn't want to take any chances.

After the exposure experiment with Quinn failed — when Rob tried to get him to say that Grandpa wasn't coming back — Rob tried getting him simply to walk across the living room into the dining room and not backtrack. Quinn was still doing this backtracking every day, walking into a room and leaving the exact way he'd entered, as if there were invisible footsteps on the floor that he had to retrace. Quinn said that the anxiety level of not retracing his steps was only a three out of five. On the chart he and Rob had made, all the other behaviours were still rated as fives, which meant they were too anxiety-inducing to tackle yet.

"So how did he do?" I asked.

"He lasted forty-five seconds in the dining room. He was just standing there with his back to me and making weird noises, like it was painful. Then he backtracked into the living room again." Even though Rob looked exhausted, his eyes were shining.

"But why do you look so happy?" I asked. "That doesn't sound that great."

"It's a breakthrough. It's the first behaviour we've found in all this time that he can actually work on. And he lasted a full forty-five seconds. I finally figured out that these are the behaviours we should work on first because he has a way out if he needs it. He knows he can always backtrack. He just needs to stay in the dining room as long as he can and then he can retrace his steps. I told him if he can stay in the dining room a full two minutes tomorrow we'll play cars together. He liked that idea."

"And the picture on his wall? Can you work on that? Or what about just taking it down and hiding it?" I knew my suggestion sounded crass and unhelpful. Taking down that picture might send him over the edge. I sighed. "Maybe not a good idea," I added.

"And one day he'll have to see that picture hanging there where it's always been hanging and not feel he has to touch it and talk to your dad." Rob's expression forwarded itself to someplace far away. I knew what he was thinking, the same thing I was thinking: that day seemed a long way off.

CHAPTER 14

The next morning I was in the kitchen with Quinn as I doled him out various remedies that supposedly helped lower anxiety and increase the serotonin to his brain. (Experts believe that OCD is related to the brain's natural flow of serotonin being blocked.) I was giving him inositol and something called 5-HTP, a naturally occurring amino acid to help boost serotonin levels, along with B vitamins and calcium and magnesium for the anxiety. A lot of the information I was getting from books and from a friend of mine who was a nurse urged us to put Quinn on antidepressants. Antidepressants are commonly prescribed to people with OCD, not to stop the compulsions but to get the anxiety level low enough for cognitive behaviour therapy to work. So far we'd been relying on the cognitive behaviour therapy alone. I'd read so many frightening stories on OCD forums about kids and antidepressants that I was vehemently hoping we wouldn't have to drug him. Besides, I was terrified of antidepressants.

A few months before Rob and I were married, in the spring of 2001, one of my very best friends in the world, Joe Fisher, committed suicide by jumping off a cliff. I blame his death on antidepressants.

I'd first met Joe when he taught a creative non-fiction class and I was his student. In Joe Fisher's presence people felt alive, as if for the hours you were with him, there was nowhere else in the world to be and nothing else to do but listen to Joe's stories. He once told me that when he was twenty-five he had gone to a Caribbean island and met a fisherman who took him on a rickety boat.

When a storm blew in, the boat capsized and the two men nearly drowned. Water began to fill Joe's lungs and an eerie surrender crept over him. Just then a dark muscled arm reached into the water, gathered him up, and threw him into a boat. When the rescue crew dumped Joe and the fisherman on shore, Joe dropped to his knees, kissed the ground, and then ran down the beach as if in a dream. Everything had taken on an aching vibrancy. "I'm alive! I'm alive!" he had shouted. An island woman watched him with amusement. They met, fell into an ecstatic love, and spent a week of what he called "being alive" together.

Joe was a journalist, a poet, an extensive world traveller, and the best-selling author of eight books, including *The Case for Reincarnation*, with a foreword by the Dalai Lama. One of his special interests was metaphysics and reincarnation, and here lies the irony: He considered suicide an injunction against cosmic law because those who commit it return to face the same problems in their next life. A chapter in one of his books was titled "The Fallacy of Suicide." Yet on a sunny afternoon in May, Joe jumped off a cliff into the Elora Gorge near Guelph. His death sent shock waves through our community of friends, slashing through the hearts of the many who loved him. Joe was always the life of the party, always so upbeat and fun, we all said. How could this be possible?

The contributing circumstances were that just as Joe had been recovering from a serious back operation following a year of pain, he was faced with a financial crisis concerning land he'd bought in his beloved Prince Edward County, Ontario. These events coincided with his coming off painkillers cold turkey, then, ten days before he died, going to a doctor who gave him a sample bottle of untested antidepressants. Joe never knew this — it wasn't printed on the bottle — but one of the side effects of those antidepressants was "suicidal tendencies."

Perhaps for people who actually have a chemical imbalance and suffer from real depression, antidepressants are a good idea. But to prescribe them to someone normally happy and only temporarily going through a tough time seemed appalling. I've been wary of antidepressants ever since.

As for Quinn, he did seem depressed as I watched him swallow those natural remedies. But I knew it was the OCD that was causing it. The real Quinn was a bright-eyed, naturally exuberant boy full of fun, and, like Joe, a sensitive soul. I was willing to do everything in my power to protect him and bring him back to himself, and to me, unless things got so bad that it was our only option, that wasn't going to involve putting him on drugs.

CHAPTER 15

EMAIL TO QUINN'S SCOUT LEADER

Hi Susan,

I'm sorry but I don't think Quinn can go camping with the Scouts this weekend after all. We're dealing with something that has come out of left field. Quinn has developed OCD and is anxious about all kinds of things that were no big deal to him a few months ago. I know the old Quinn loved Cubs and was looking forward to Scouts. Considering that he was full of anxiety just from being at his aunt's recently (who he normally loves visiting) we can't risk his going camping. I'm so sorry this is all happening!

Yours truly,
Laurie

Sometime during Quinn's first missed week of school, he stopped talking, at least in full sentences. He was sitting next to me on the couch one morning, lost in a trance, mumbling to himself. My iPad lay on the coffee table and I suddenly wondered why he didn't play Minecraft on it any more. This was the only video game he played, or at least, used to play. I hadn't seen him playing it in weeks. Normally I didn't like him wasting so much time on the game and always encouraged him to read instead. However, he used to enjoy Minecraft so much that I thought playing it again now would restore some of his former joy, or at least bring him out of his zombie state. "Hey, Quinn, Earth to Quinn! Do you want to play Minecraft?" He was so far off in another galaxy I was practically shouting as I handed him the tablet. He didn't even look at me when he answered.

"Can't, can't. Too hard now. Now hard, too."

I blinked. "What?"

Staring out the window, he said, "Have to erase everything. Everything erase to have."

"Are you talking backward?"

"I'm erasing. Erasing I'm."

"Jesus Christ. Why are you doing that, Quinn?"

He kept staring out the window at a red squirrel running the length of our railing on the deck. "Have to. To have."

"You're erasing your words? And that's why you don't play Minecraft any more? You'd have to erase what you created?"

He nodded, then turned to look right at me in alarm, like he had no idea why any of this was happening to him, like he was lost in a deep, tangled forest and he wanted me to help him find his way out.

But how to find my way in?

"Oh, sweetie," I said, "it's going to be okay. You're going to get better. This won't last forever. I promise."

He grabbed a cushion from beside him on the couch and hurled it across the living room. "I hate OCD!" he shouted.

"Me, too!" I threw a cushion across the room also. "I hate your OCD bully! He's an asshole!"

"Yeah!" said Quinn, brightening.

I snatched the cushion behind me and tossed it at Quinn. "Let's have a pillow fight!" He looked at me in surprise and I could see the tiniest of smiles curling the line of his mouth. "Go get more pillows from your room. We'll collect all the pillows in the house!" Quinn stood up as if he were on the way to get the pillows. Then he sat down again.

"What? Aren't you getting them? It'll be fun! You and Halla always used to have pillow fights. And you and I did, too. Remember? We can pretend our orange chair is the OCD bully and beat it with pillows. We can even kick it. Punch it!"

He was back to staring out the window. "Can't, can't."

The second *can't* was almost whispered, to erase having said it the first time, I guessed. A great anger was swelling up in me. Who the hell did this OCD bully think he was, kidnapping my lovely little boy like this? Holding him hostage? Ruining his life?

"I so fucking can't stand that OCD bully!" I heard myself say. "Why is he doing this to us?" At that moment I didn't care that I was swearing in front of my child. Everything felt hopeless. "I feel like turning you upside-down by the ankles and shaking the OCD out of you. Can I?" I tickled him in the ribs. "Can I, sweetie?"

Quinn looked at me with a face that seemed to have resigned from duty. He was far away again, about to become as remote and unfathomable as interstellar space. "Wouldn't work." He turned his gaze back to outside. In a smaller voice, he said, "Work wouldn't."

That afternoon I took Quinn to what would be the first of two appointments with a hypnotherapist in the nearby Quebec town of Aylmer. When you have an unwell child you will try almost anything to get him better, even if it goes against your better judgment. Just the day before, Rob had blurted out, "Let's just pack the camper van and head for the Southwest. We can stay in the desert at one of those National Forest campgrounds. We can go back to that extreme mountain bike place that Quinn loved. He'll have no time for OCD if he's riding his bike on a course like that every day." I thought back to our camping trip from two years before and the bike ride we'd done, the exhilarating wind-roaring climbs up into the Colorado blue sky before the terrifying plummet back down over the red rock ground. Still, I knew it wouldn't work. This was the kind of escapist thinking I'm usually prone to myself. I was surprised to hear it coming from rational Rob. I told him going there would just mean we'd have a child with OCD in the desert instead of here. He saw my point.

But now, here I was doing something perhaps equally desperate, calling a hypnotist. I'd first called this woman back in the summer, when Quinn was evening-off and I didn't yet understand it was OCD. I'd thought perhaps hypnotism could stop the behaviour. We'd had a long conversation, and this woman had explained in a sweet voice that she believed in something called family constellations. She was convinced that when people are emotionally stuck, it's the result of a trauma in the life of one of his or her ancestors. I found this fascinating but it didn't jive with Quinn's situation. His problem was clearly his own personal trauma of losing his grandpa; forget trauma in the lives of his ancestors. And anyway, doesn't everyone on the planet have ancestors who experienced some kind of trauma and loss? A century ago people simply accepted that terrible things could happen to them at any time because they so often did. Nonetheless, when I'd explained about Quinn making everything even, she told me treating something like that would be easy for her, especially since he was a kid. I didn't make an appointment with her back then because he had actually improved over the summer, and, besides, she sounded a little flaky and overconfident. But now, when the OCD was so much worse than in those early days of simply making things even, and since we were still on in those interminable waiting lists with the medical system, I'd called her again. When I explained the situation this time, she was surprisingly still full of confidence. She told me she'd gotten rid of children's OCD many times. "I can probably do it in one session."

"But wait," I said. "If OCD is so easily curable through hypnotism, why doesn't everyone with OCD do it?"

"Because people think it's too out there, too unscientific."

"But people with OCD, and parents with kids with OCD, will try anything. We're desperate," I told her. "That's how I feel right now. If it really worked to cure OCD, wouldn't people be shouting it from the rooftops? It would be a massive breakthrough." As it was, I couldn't find any research claiming hypnotism worked for OCD at all. Nothing. Still, I was calling her anyway.

"It works ninety-three percent of the time," she stated. "And cognitive behaviour therapy only works twenty-eight percent of the time."

I felt like asking her where she was getting her statistics. Perhaps I should have hung up right then, but, instead, I made an appointment with her, which shows my level of despair at the time. It was easy to get an appointment right away, which maybe should have told me something.

On the drive to Aylmer, Quinn rolled down the window five separate times to stick his head out in the wind, put his hand on his heart, and ask his grandpa to come back.

"I think this woman might be able to help you, Quinn," I said, between bouts of window unwinding. "You know how I've been telling you that story about running on the beach at night and it helps you relax and sleep? I think this woman will do something like that, only better. She sounded really nice on the phone."

Quinn just stared out the window at the passing trees of Gatineau Park. The leaves were drifting down like broken feathers in the wind, while all around us the colour was leaching from the landscape.

The hypnotherapist held her sessions in her split-level house in a seventies-era suburban neighbourhood where the wide Ottawa River was so close you could hear its waves lapping ashore. After we met her in the front hall and talked a little, she took Quinn into her living room and asked me to come back in forty-five minutes. I waited in the car and read an old *National Geographic* I found in the back seat. When I came back, she asked to talk to me in private. Quinn went out to the car.

"I think it went really well," she said excitedly.

"Really? That's fantastic!"

"I got him into a relaxed state, then got him to choose these plastic foot shapes from a basket." She pointed to some coloured insoles lined up in her living room. "I asked him to choose a pair of feet for himself, then pairs of feet for the people in his life that he's closest to. I got him to line these feet up next to each other. He put your dad's feet next to his, then yours, your husband's, and your mother's were all next to your dad's. Then I got him to stand on his own coloured feet and say how he felt. He spoke to your dad and said he wanted him back. Then I got him to stand on your dad's feet and talk in your dad's voice. When he stood on these big feet of your dad's, he said, 'Quinn, I want you to be the happy Quinn you always were, who loves soccer and running and riding your unicycle. Happy.'"

"That's amazing," I said. "That sounds like a really cool technique." I felt like I could finally breathe. I hadn't felt this kind of lightness in a long time.

She continued, saying that when she tried to get Quinn to move his foot shapes forward, and do the same with mine and Rob's, he didn't want to do it. He didn't want to leave Grandpa's feet behind. "So I told him, 'Quinn,

Grandpa isn't happy. He's having trouble moving on to where he needs to go because you keep calling him back.' After a while, he finally moved the feet forward. I think you'll see a huge change in him now."

"That's brilliant," I said. "I'm so grateful!"

"Yeah, I learned that technique from my teacher. He's a genius." Her eyes were like two shiny pennies.

After paying her $125 cash, I couldn't wait to get out to the car to see Quinn.

JOURNAL

I'm sitting on an outdoor bench on this chilly evening while Quinn is practising soccer drills with his teammates. They're running around in T-shirts despite the cold. We just came from Aylmer. Even from this distance I can still see Quinn doing his usual OCD jerking movements. I was so hoping the hypnotherapy worked. But maybe it did work a little on some level. At the very least it might have worked as grief counselling. As soon as we started the car and got back on the road toward home, he rolled down the window to start the same old routine. I felt my heart slide right into my feet. I wonder if I should tell the hypnotherapist. She seemed pretty convinced she'd cured him.

Two teenage girls are having a conversation in French beside me. They're looking at their phones and laughing. I have that feeling I've had before when you see people going on about their normal lives and you realize you're not one of them anymore, that the fabric of your life has a hole in it. It seems impossible to understand how the people around you can feel happiness and laugh. People have no idea how easily broken life is, how it can all change on a dime. You blink and then when you look at the world again you've lost your bearings.

CHAPTER 16

That week, I came across a YouTube video of a Dr. Phil show called "Inside the World of OCD." The first part of the video was so disturbing I kept hitting the pause button. It took me three tries before I finally got through the whole thing. It showed footage of a young man who I kept thinking could be Quinn one day. This guy regularly goes in and out of OCD trances and can barely function — his whole life has been crippled by OCD — while his poor parents watch helplessly, hoping for a miracle. Then Dr. Phil introduced a neuroradiologist named Dr. Jabour who runs a clinic in Los Angeles and treats people with OCD. He uses something called transcranial magnetic stimulation, which is supposedly a non-invasive procedure that sends magnetic impulses to the brain to stimulate certain neurons associated with OCD. He's had a lot of success curing people. I was so buoyed by the video that I sent Dr. Jabour an email asking if we could fly Quinn out there to try it. Not long after I sent the email, a woman from Dr. Jabour's clinic called to say that they don't treat people until they're at least sixteen because their brains haven't fully developed yet.

JOURNAL

> I'm walking along River Road again tonight. Now when I look
> up into the stars, I get no comfort whatsoever. No worries are

taken away, there are no eternities to fall into. At this moment, I feel so crushed by the weight of the sky that I can't imagine life ever getting better again. I want to fall into a black hole.

The email from Dr. Jabour's office dashed another hope today. This whole journey is such an emotional roller coaster. I keep getting moments of false hope where it seems like things will be okay again — when Quinn actually goes through several OCD-free minutes — but then the shock of reality hits when I see he's come up with something new. Tonight he refused dessert — he never refuses dessert — because he told himself if he ate it, Grandpa wouldn't come back. And then yet another new behaviour: clenching his fists into tight balls. Even my trying to put him into the relaxed state before bed isn't working any more. And forget reading to him at night now, which I've been doing ever since he was a baby. How could he even hear me when he's talking to my dad while I'm trying to read?

I would gladly give up every single possession I own, toss it all away without a thought, give away our home with everything in it, if it meant getting Quinn back. I'd happily walk barefoot and homeless down this road if I could walk with a carefree, healthy Quinn.

I'm learning I have to enjoy the hopeful moments when they come, otherwise what do I have? I've always been a naturally optimistic person. People have often described me as fun and exuberant, full of happy, infectious energy. But I can't even remember that person right now. This is a test beyond anything I've ever endured. This makes teaching on the native reserve on James Bay when I was twenty-five a cakewalk. This makes Quinn's colic followed by two years of sleep deprivation a joke. I'd kill to go back to that time. What's a little lost sleep? I remember feeling desperate when I was twenty and hitchhiking in Oregon. I was so lost and aimless that I didn't know which side of the road to stand on to get a ride, whether I should go north to my old life or south to a new one. If only I'd known something like this would come someday, something truly hard. On second thought, I wouldn't have wanted to know that.

I stop walking to gaze up at the zillions of cold-hearted stars pinpricking the sky. Will Quinn ever look up this far into the night sky or will he be a child with a starless universe?

Oh, God, if you're out there, please hear me: I want my son back.

At times I've prayed to a God I was hoping, against all evidence and logic, somehow existed. This can happen even to atheists when we're trudging through the emotional trenches. In times of crisis, like now, I've fallen back to my childhood notion of God, whom I came to love when I was eight. This happened to me because for a few years as a kid, I went to church by myself, a lone believer in a family of agnostics. I went because I wanted to be in the church choir with my best friend Julie. Singing was fun, no matter that I wasn't a very good singer. One year we got to perform *Joseph and the Amazing Technicolor Dreamcoat* and I sang the lyrics at home continually, annoying my sister so much that she used to kick me under the kitchen table to shut me up. I even went to a church camp where our born-again seventeen-year-old counsellor, Joni, told me I better get my parents to invite Jesus into their hearts or they wouldn't be going to heaven. This kept me up at night. I thought my mom would be okay since she'd gone to church as a kid so probably at some point had invited Jesus into her heart even though she'd forgotten he was in there. But I was sure my dad had never done any inviting of that kind. I decided that when I got home, I'd work on my dad in a religious sense, get him to see the light. I remember tiptoeing into his room one morning, leaning down next to him as he slept, and whispering, "Jesus, come into my heart. Come in, Jesus. I invite you in." I'd learned about subliminal advertising and brainwashing in school and I thought my dad might start dreaming the words I was whispering and that would be good enough for Jesus. "Jesus," I whispered a little louder, "you're welcome in my heart. Come in, please." I kept that up for a while until my dad made a grunting noise and his eyes flew open. I recall him asking what I was doing. "Just, you know, nothing really," I answered.

I don't remember when I stopped believing in God. It must have been a gradual awakening over the years, deprogramming from those early years of going to church, and learning science instead. I remember once hiking in British Columbia's interior, searching for a cabin at the trail's end. After a few hours I lost the trail in the suddenly deep June snow. Somehow I ended up on an icy mountainside where one wrong move and I'd tumble to my death into a canyon. As I traversed the treacherously steep snowfield in my running shoes, I heard myself suddenly crying out, "Please, God, please God," over and over. When I made it to the other side intact I felt an ecstatic kind of bliss that maybe only occurs in that sort of situation. I wonder if I'd have prayed like that if I hadn't gone to church as a kid. Likely not. But in those few moments it really did feel like I wasn't alone, that I was calling out to my childhood God. Later, I would learn that the same parts of the brain are active when you pray as when you're interacting with other people, so of course it "feels" as if someone is there. Also, perhaps this feeling was the result of millions of years of evolution, and that those who believed in gods passed on those genes because believing in gods helped us survive. It's an enormous comfort to believe in the magic of a god.

I needed some of that magical comfort in my life again. "Please, God," I'd whisper into the dark at 3:00 a.m. some nights in bed. "Please let Quinn be okay. Please." Although every time I'd say this I was met with the eerie feeling that my prayer wasn't so different from Quinn uttering, "Please come back."

Magical thinking was all around me that fall.

CHAPTER 17

"Should we race, Quinn?" asked my friend Stephan as the three of us pedalled our bikes along a path into Gatineau Park. Every time Stephan visited
us from northern Ontario, we'd go for at least one major bike ride. Quinn
always loved it, tearing ahead of us over the dirt trails, flying down steep
wooded hills, getting his legs scratched up by blackberry bushes, negotiating
hairpin curves that I'd never consider except by foot.

"Yes!"shouted Quinn. I watched as the two of them sped ahead, and
gripped my handlebars tighter than usual, watching to see if the OCD bully
was anywhere nearby. So far, biking fast through the woods seemed to be
like soccer, exhilarating enough and demanding enough concentration that
OCD had no space to get in — Rob had recently set up a unicycle obstacle
course in our yard because he'd noticed that when Quinn rode the unicycle
it required so much focus that his OCD bully couldn't mess with him.

It also helped to have Stephan visiting: Quinn had always loved him like
an uncle. Stephan and I had been friends since we'd met at teachers' college
years earlier. I'd told Stephan about Quinn's OCD in emails, but somehow
I had gotten the feeling that he thought I was exaggerating. How could
someone as stable, calm, and drama-free as Quinn ever acquire such a thing?

It didn't take long for Stephan to see I wasn't exaggerating. After half
an hour on the trail, we realized that Quinn had fallen behind. "That's
weird," said Stephan. "Since when does this ever happen? What's he doing
back there?"

"I hate to think," I said. "I'll go check." When I rode back I could see Quinn just standing there on the trail beside his bike, not moving.

"Are you having trouble, Quinn? We'll be at Brown Lake soon. Let's keep going."

He gave me a distressed look but got on his bike anyway. He pedalled for about twenty seconds before getting off again. "I have to go back the same way I came," he suddenly blurted out.

"No, you don't," I called back. "That's the OCD bully telling you that. He wants to ruin your day. Boss him back! Tell him you're going to Brown Lake with your mother and Stephan!"

He got back on his bike and tried again, pedalling a little longer this time. Then I heard a crash. I turned around and saw that Quinn had thrown his bike into a bush. He was standing with his arms crossed and a fierce look of loathing on his face. "I hate this!" he shrieked. "I fucking hate this! I wish I was dead!"

"What's going on?" said Stephan. He'd ridden back when he'd heard the commotion and was now watching Quinn. For the briefest of moments I caught a glimmer of unmasked fear on Stephan's face, then it was gone. "I can't wait to plunge into Brown Lake. How about you, Quinn?"

Quinn's bike was still in the bush. "Stephan is crazy, isn't he, Quinn? Swimming in October? Do you think he'll really do it?"

"Laurie, I've gone swimming in October at Brown Lake before. I'd do it in November if someone paid me a hundred dollars. What about you, Quinn? How much would someone have to pay you to swim in November?"

Quinn appeared to be thinking about this. I could see the struggle on his face, and his wanting desperately to keep riding his bike with us, while the OCD monster was demanding he go back the way he came, to erase the fun he'd had so far.

"Brown Lake! Let's go!" I suddenly shouted. I motioned for Stephan to get going. Stephan and I would ride to the lake no matter what. We weren't going to enable the OCD bully and go back the way we'd come. Quinn would have to make the choice himself. He'd have to see how much OCD was wrecking his life.

Even if I hadn't read that this was actually what we were supposed to be doing — refusing to enable the OCD — I knew down into my bone marrow it was the right thing to do. Still, it felt cruel. What mother leaves her child alone in the woods? Even if he was ten and perfectly capable of riding back to Wakefield on his own by the same trail — and I knew he'd take the exact same trail since the whole point was to backtrack — I was a little panicked. I thought he'd follow us but wasn't totally sure.

Stephan and I kept riding toward the lake. After a few minutes he stopped on the trail to say, "Jesus, Laurie, I'm sorry. I didn't really believe you about this. He's like a completely different kid. That's not the Quinn I know at all. That really scared me back there."

"It scares me every day." Neither of us spoke for a while. I was trying to remember that other Quinn, the one Stephan remembered. I recalled how funny Quinn used to be, how he liked talking in British accents, pretending when he set the table to be the snobby butler on *Downton Abbey*, or using a cockney accent to discuss various race cars or cars he'd see on the street. *Blimey, that's a beater innit?*

"Hey, look!" said Stephan. "He's coming."

I turned around and saw the red splash of Quinn's shirt soaring at us through the jack pines. I took in a deep thankful breath.

"Yippee, Quinn! You did it! Way to go!" I shouted.

Quinn flashed me the briefest of smiles and passed us on the trail. My heart leapt like a gazelle that the day could continue and he'd fought back the bully. Soon, we arrived at the place where we always leave our bikes propped against some hemlocks before heading down to the lake. We live in a mixed northern forest and sometimes we'd come across stone walls, cellar holes, and evidence of previous habitations — old apple orchards, for instance — right in the middle of the woods or meadows, places where a few generations of hardy immigrants toiled to clear the land and farm only to eventually admit defeat and abandon the enterprise. To get to Brown Lake after we park our bikes, we always walk down some crumbling stone steps that I imagine some Irish farmer built over a century ago.

"These steps are still here," said Quinn to Stephan, knowing that Stephan is interested in this sort of thing — he's a member of a tribe that could be known as "explorers of the undiscovered country of the nearby." I noticed Quinn's mood had perked up. I also noticed he was tightly clutching something that looked like a little stick in his fist. This was a behaviour he was still doing a lot, holding on to pebbles and sticks, not wanting to let things go. Then it hit me: he'd probably picked the stick up back where he'd thrown his bike into the bush. It was an OCD bargain — *I won't backtrack this time but I'll hold on to this stick. That way, Grandpa can still come back.*

When we got to our favourite swimming rock beside the lake, Stephan rolled up his sleeve, stuck his arm in the water, and swished it around. "Nope. Won't be swimming today." The sky was a milky blue and a breeze floated softly off the water. The quiet all around us seemed like a pause before winter's frozen iron teeth would start to bite.

"Quinn," I said, when we were all sitting on the rock. "What do you think about throwing that stick into the water?"

Quinn shook his head and scooted back a couple of feet, as if he were afraid I'd grab the stick out of his hand. "No!" His face was resolute and frightened.

"It might feel really good. You'd be setting it free," I offered. I threw a crumpled leaf into the water. "See? Now that leaf gets to go for a ride around the lake, on its own little journey."

He kept shaking his head, clutching the stick tighter. "Quinn," said Stephan, taking his phone out of his pocket. "I want to show you a picture." He started clicking through photos. When he found what he was looking for, he said, "I can see you're having a hard time letting your grandpa go. That's why you don't want to let go of things, like that stick." Quinn didn't say anything but I could tell he was listening. "See this picture?" Quinn leaned over to study Stephan's phone. "It's a bench in the woods. When my dad died we bought this special bench and put it in the woods overlooking a lake. We put a plaque on the bench with my dad's name on it. Now when I want to talk to my dad, I go for a walk in the woods to that bench. I sit down on it and tell him things. I tell him about my girlfriend, what's going on in the world, the price of gas now, that kind of thing."

"Really?" asked Quinn, still looking at the picture.

"Yep, I go every so often, just to chat, at least once a season." Quinn seemed to be opening a little. I could see he was contemplating what Stephan had said, wondering perhaps why Stephan didn't ask his dad to come back.

Finally, I said, "You could just toss that stick in the lake and say goodbye to it. Or what about breaking it in half and just throwing part of it away?"

Quinn shook his head. After twenty minutes or so of Stephan and my trying to convince him, Quinn interrupted to say, "Okay, I'll do it! But I won't throw it in the water. I'll bury it right here and then come back for it sometime."

We cheered for him as he dug a place for the little stick. *I guess this is as good as it gets today*, I thought. Stephan seemed overjoyed, but he didn't know what I knew, that burying the stick still allowed for a way to undo what he'd done, to come and find it another day if he had to. Setting it free into the water was irreversible: it meant letting go.

Quinn was almost his old self again that evening. It seemed that what had happened at the lake had affected him, worn away some of the turtle shell he'd built around himself. He even announced that he was going to school the next day, a Friday. I couldn't believe it.

The next morning he'd changed his mind about school, but did say he'd like to try going just for the half-hour lunch recess so he could play soccer. Stephan, Quinn, and I rode our bikes up to the school. We got to the edge of the playground, to the top of a little bike path in the trees, just as the recess bell sounded. Soon, Quinn saw his friends rushing outside and starting to kick the ball around. He took a deep breath and said, "I'm doing this!" then ran to the field to join them. Stephan and I hung back in the trees, quietly astounded he'd actually gone through with it.

"Aren't his friends going to find it weird that he missed this whole week of school and now just shows up for recess?" asked Stephan.

"They're boys. Boys don't ask questions like that. They just want to play soccer. Girls would be more curious. Hey, look!" I pointed at the field, where Quinn suddenly had control of the ball and was racing toward the net. "He's playing like the old Quinn!" We both watched in wonder. The playground came breathing to life in saturated greens and blues. I couldn't believe the happiness that bloomed inside me when I heard his friends shout, "Quinn, pass! Quinn, over here!" The half-hour recess felt like an unexpected act of grace tossed down from the sky. On the little soccer pitch filled with sweaty ten-year-old boys, life was the way it always had been. No OCD bullies allowed.

"Geez, when I was a kid," said Stephan, "we didn't play soccer like these kids do now. We didn't do any of that fancy footwork. We just kicked the ball."

I agreed and it felt good to be discussing something other than OCD for a change. When the bell rang, Quinn didn't return right away. Ten minutes later he showed up with a half-eaten piece of pizza. "Pizza day," he said as he chewed. "I thought I'd go inside and get mine."

I looked at him with a crooked smile. "And your friends, what did they think about you just showing up like that for recess?"

He popped the last of the pizza into his mouth and brushed the tomato sauce from his cheek. "They said I was lucky to skip school and just come for soccer and pizza." He giggled. The three of us rode our bikes back home laughing.

That afternoon I picked my friend Chantal up from the airport. We were having a girls' night that evening at another friend's house. Chantal and her family had temporarily moved out west and now she had a few days free to visit on her own. We went to lunch in Ottawa at a vegetarian restaurant we loved called The Green Door. I'd emailed her about Quinn but I didn't think she'd understood. When I started to give examples of what Quinn's OCD looked like — he has to hop across the living room floor on one foot, or unroll the car window to stick his head out and start asking his grandpa to come back — she started laughing, howling actually. I immediately recognized it as nervous hysteria. I myself had fallen victim to this many times in my life in uncomfortable situations. Watching Chantal laugh got me laughing hysterically, too. The two of us just kept laughing like baboons in the restaurant as everyone around us looked on in dismay. "This is my life now," I kept saying between gasps. "This is my life."

It was lucky timing I'd had the break of a girls' night on Friday, because what happened on Saturday night flew up straight from hell and landed in our living room.

Rob was out, having volunteered to work the sound equipment at the community centre, so Quinn and I were alone that evening. I thought we could watch *Portlandia* on my iPad while we sat together on the couch. Just as the show got going, Quinn shut his eyes. "What are you doing?" I asked.

"I can't open my eyes. If I open them, Grandpa won't come back."

"Quinn, that's the OCD bully. You can do it. You can open your eyes."

"I can't!" he shouted.

His long-lashed eyes stayed closed. "But how can you watch the show? We could make popcorn, too. Just open your eyes."

He shook his head. "Sometimes I keep my eyes open without blinking. This at least feels better."

"Oh, God, Quinn. I didn't know you kept your eyes open without blinking."

"I only did it once."

"That's really bad for your eyes. Don't do it again, please."

"Okay," he said quietly.

I spent the next hour pleading with him to open his eyes, trying everything I could think of, even watching funny videos on YouTube and laughing out loud, saying, "That's hilarious! Oh, my God, I can't believe that just happened! You have to see this!" He kept his eyes closed the entire time. It must have been an incredible strength of will, even harder than forgoing dessert.

Finally, just as I was about to give up, he opened his eyes for the briefest of moments and looked at me, revealing two gleaming, red-rimmed eyes full of fear. Then he closed them again. He didn't open them again for the rest of the night. He brushed his teeth with his eyes closed, swallowed his remedies with water, and knocked into walls before finally climbing up the ladder to his bunk bed, where he flopped down, defeated and miserable. I climbed up onto the bed next to him and gathered him in my arms. I sang him "Moon River" and "Hush, Little Baby" and every song I could think of that I used to sing to him when he was little. After singing I whispered, "I just want you to get better, Quinn. I love you so much." I started sobbing, saying over and over again that I loved him and I wanted him back. He cried, too. I was holding him so hard, the sad lost echo of my son. I kept telling him how much I loved him until he fell asleep.

As he slept I thought back to another time I'd held him, back to when he was less than a week old. We were lying in bed together in the early morning winter light. I remember thinking this was the first time the sun had come out since his birth and its snow-bright rays were flooding through the window above us. I noticed Quinn's eyes were suddenly wide open, and they seemed to be in utter awe of his surroundings. I moved closer, so my forehead was touching his tiny one. I was entranced. He seemed to be taking in both me and the world for the very first time and I was there to witness it. I realized this was his first look at life and he was enraptured. The surge of love and sensation I felt was nearly unbearable. I was there for the moment when the world opened itself up to Quinn, or he opened up to it, which simultaneously meant the world opened itself up to me. All that time in the womb, I thought, and he had no idea that any of this was waiting for him out here: the warm sunlight on his cheeks, dancing shadows of the swaying trees, his mother's eyes staring back at him. The moment was so fragile that I was almost afraid to breathe for fear of it shattering. I'd never felt so deeply connected to another human being, so much so that I was seeing through his eyes, getting a glimpse into another reality, one much more alive and true than the one I normally inhabited. Something inside me had cracked wide open and in an instant I had surfaced into a larger beauty. I will never forget that moment. It's the moment I hope to savour someday when I'm down to my last few minutes of life.

How can a mother or father ever hold on to the space and time that their child passes through so fleetingly? How to halt time?

CHAPTER 18

What happened the next day, on Sunday, didn't take on significance until later. At the time, I wasn't sure what to think. Quinn was no longer keeping his eyes shut like the night before, but he wasn't talking, either. He'd been shrouded in a dome of silence all morning. I thought it was because it was one of his days where he told himself he had to erase his sentences and say all the words backward, and those days were too taxing on his brain. Around noon, I called him for lunch but I couldn't find him. I thought perhaps he was upstairs with Rob doing the ERP exercises. But Rob was alone. I went back downstairs and checked again in his bedroom. I noticed his window was open, a breeze playing at the curtain. I realized he'd climbed out his window. I went outside. When I got there I noticed how wild and overgrown my garden had become. I hadn't realized how much I'd been neglecting it. That's when I heard the singing. I looked around but couldn't see its source. I started walking down our laneway. The singing got louder. I kept walking. Now I could clearly hear Quinn singing but couldn't see him anywhere. When I got to the end of our laneway, I looked up. Quinn was at the very top of our pine tree. It was the same white pine he'd been climbing earlier in the fall at sunset to ask my dad to come back. When he saw me he stopped singing and called out, "Hi, Mummy!" and started climbing down. He jumped off one of the lower branches and landed in front of me. His face was flushed pink. I asked what he'd been doing, saying, "Hey, Quinn, what's up?"

In a steady strong voice, looking me in the eyes, he said, "I sang 'Somewhere Over the Rainbow' to Grandpa and I let him go."

I stared at him. A blue jay squawked nearby. "You what?"

"I sang the whole song. Then I let him go." He said this matter-of-factly. He was smiling. There was a calmness in his face I hadn't seen in weeks. He began walking up the lane, saying he didn't want to be late for soccer. I stood there watching him as he made his way up the laneway kicking a stone like a soccer ball. I cast my eyes up to the top of the pine tree and heard a faint whistling wind deep in its leaves. *Could it be true?* I was so tired of false hopes that all I could do was take in the moment and whisper a hushed prayer up into the tree: *Please.*

He was quiet during the whole drive to the indoor soccer field in Hull. I didn't see him displaying any OCD on the way there or at soccer itself. I felt like I was holding my breath the entire time. But when soccer was over and we were walking back to the car, he suddenly stopped walking with us. *Damn,* I thought, *he's stuck. I knew it was too good to be true.* Although he was only dressed in shorts and his soccer jersey when he should have been wearing a warm jacket, he still took ten minutes to move forward from his frozen place in the parking lot.

Later, he and I were waiting in the car while Rob picked something up at a grocery store on Rideau Street. He was quiet for a long time. Finally, he said, "Mummy, do you think I'm still trying to get Grandpa back?"

I turned around. He was playing with the laces of his soccer cleats but kept glancing up at me. "Um, yes? Maybe? Are you?"

"No. I let him go up in the tree." He paused. "But now I want something else." He looked partly excited, partly wary, like he was letting me in on a big secret.

"You want something else? What?"

"To win the Olympics. To win a big race."

"Huh? What race? When?"

"When I'm older."

Was he switching obsessions? He obviously still had OCD. Getting stuck in the parking lot confirmed that. What was going on?

"Quinn, it would be fantastic to train to be a runner one day. But that sounds like it's still your OCD bully telling you that. I'm so happy that you let Grandpa go, that's such a huge thing you did! And I'm so proud of you!

But the OCD still seems to be stuck in your brain a little bit. You have to fight the bully harder than ever. You're almost there!"

He sighed in a way that only adults should sigh and looked out at the homeless people walking by on Rideau Street. Meanwhile, I was trying to figure out where winning the Olympics came from. It seemed so out of the blue, so unlike Quinn to want something like that. My dad was a track runner so there was a vague connection, but still, it was a bizarre.

On Monday his new obsession had grown in power. He lay paralyzed on the couch the entire afternoon because if he spoke or moved a muscle he wouldn't win the Olympics. I was looking after Anna's five-year-old son, who kept trying to tickle Quinn and get him to play. It seemed like it could have been therapeutic, like a little puppy trying to spark a reaction, but Quinn just kept lying there, almost comatose. When Anna came to pick up her son and saw Quinn in that state I realized nobody outside of Rob and me had seen him this way. He was so shot through with OCD that it was frightening. Luckily, she's a therapist so she knew how to react. Or maybe she knew how to react because of the caring person she is. I don't even remember what she said, only that she tried to talk to Quinn and smile at both of us and tell me she'd help however she could. Her brief visit was like opening a window into our house to let in some fresh air.

EMAIL, OCTOBER 21, 2013

Hi Tina,

I don't know how much more I can take. Quinn is in freefall. I told him tonight I'd be happy if a nuclear bomb dropped down on us and we were all killed. In the stilted way he talks now he said he'd like that, too. This is the kind of thing Rob would never say to Quinn. I can't believe these things come out of my mouth sometimes. I can't imagine it's good for Quinn to hear I feel this way but sometimes it actually shakes him out of his trance. Still, it must be terrible to be a child who makes his mother feel this way, or who makes his mother cry. Some nights I wake up terrified, fear hurricaning through me with primordial force. I think, What will happen tomorrow? And, How bad will this get? I'm taking Quinn to the emergency at the children's hospital in Ottawa tomorrow. I don't care if we have to wait there all day. I won't leave until somebody sees him. This can't go on. Just when it looks like things are getting better, they get worse than I ever thought they could. I'm also going back to that hypnotherapist the day after tomorrow but I don't know if she can help. I talked to her the other day on the phone and when I told her about what happened in the tree, she said, "Oh, good, my work on him did that! It happened so quickly! Now he just needs to come one more time to finish up." I don't think she knows anything about OCD actually. She sent me this questionnaire asking about his ancestors' lives, asking if there were any murders and suicides. (There aren't that I know of but probably back there somewhere!) Did I tell you how she thinks things like OCD are from trauma passed down through our ancestors, going back as far as seven generations? Seriously. She's convinced that's where his problem lies. I'm so desperate that I feel like I have to try everything. (I even briefly considered baking Quinn some pot brownies after seeing a video of a mother in California who does this for her son with OCD. It stops his compulsions and makes him laugh, which he normally never does.)

Meanwhile, Rob is like the Rock of Gibraltar. He told everyone he works for that he can't work right now because of Quinn (which I've also done, which means zero income for the foreseeable future). Rob also gave up producing a play for Theatre Wakefield. He doesn't talk to any friends or play his guitar or build his canoe in his shop. All his energy and attention are devoted to getting Quinn better and doing ERP with him. I'm in awe of him to tell you the truth. It's incredible what a crisis can bring out in a person. I don't even think he knew he had this inside him, this unwavering dedication, this crystal-clear focus where all that matters is getting Quinn back. I remember from my years travelling that sometimes things happen to you that are shocking and scary and you end up reacting in a way that's surprising to you. You end up seeing parts of yourself that you didn't know were there, things that have never been called upon before. It's not always what you assumed was there inside you. And it's not always good. But sometimes it is. Sometimes you just have to forge ahead and do what you need to do even though everything feels hopeless. Because what else is there? But it wears you down. I'm worn down. It's really hard for me to see Quinn like this, a faint memory of the boy he was, slipping away from me by the day, the threads that tie us together as frail as a spider web. It's also hard to do those ERP exercises with him. I really suck at it, actually. It requires a level of patience that I'm learning I don't possess. Mostly, I find it emotionally devastating to see Quinn go through it all. I don't know how I'd handle this without Rob. I'm barely hanging on as it is. We're both so hollowed out we're like ghosts you can see through.

Laurie

CHAPTER 19

"Come on, sweetie. We'll be there soon. Try to just keep walking." Quinn was taking forever to walk to the children's hospital in Ottawa. I'd parked that morning in a nearby neighbourhood to avoid the hospital parking lot and now wondered if we'd ever make it there. Everything took so much more time now since Quinn was continually getting stuck or backtracking. Simple things like getting dressed and tying his shoes could take half an hour. If we showed any impatience at all he'd sense it and it made everything worse.

On arrival at the emergency wing, we were greeted at the door by a tall tree-limbed woman with purple Tina Fey glasses and hennaed red hair whose domineering stance and unsmiling face made me think she might moonlight as a bouncer. Her name tag said Olive. She asked why we were there. "My son is having some problems. OCD. It's serious. I don't know where else to go." Olive gazed down at Quinn and her previously stern face opened up like a rose in a time-lapse photography film as her smile spread out for him. After I handed over his medical card she showed us to a waiting room of couches, where a TV played soundless cartoons and a few kids were lethargically playing on the floor. Quinn didn't look at the TV — he'd never been into cartoons — and peered blankly into the middle distance as we took our chairs.

Soon, a loudspeaker voice called us into an admitting office where I explained Quinn's situation to two nurses who seemed concerned, especially since Quinn had been stuck in their office doorway for several minutes, embarrassed that he couldn't cross the threshold. I felt horrible for dragging him into this stressful, unfamiliar situation but felt I had no other choice. When Quinn finally made it into their little office, they weighed him (seventy pounds, "not an ounce of fat," they teased playfully) and took his blood pressure. Then we went back to the waiting room. While there, we watched a couple rush through the hospital entrance with their kid who'd just broken his arm playing soccer. The mother was almost hysterical as she let loose her breathless story to Olive. Clearly this couple felt the whole building should cease activity immediately to commence the repair of their kid's bent, soccer-smacked arm. I was overcome with envy. *It's only a broken arm!* I wanted to shout. *Do you know how lucky you are to have a kid with a broken arm? I'd kill for that!*

It was one of those moments when I thought, *Did I appreciate how carefree my life was before all this happened? Did I?*

Olive was having none of the broken-arm drama and made them follow the same rules as the rest of us. I felt like running over to hug her.

Two hours later another voice called us into another waiting room. This one was much smaller than the previous waiting room. It had four chairs, no windows, and what appeared to be a one-way mirror. I wondered if someone was watching us from the other side. We spent the next several hours waiting in this room. Quinn didn't stop moving for a second, continually popping up to spring his hands onto the facing wall and chant, "I will win the 2024 Olympics, one hundred metres. I will win!" The rest of the time he placed his hand on his heart and looked up at the ceiling to repeat the same mantra. Since the day he'd climbed the tree and let my dad go, he'd probably repeated this mantra one hundred times a day. It was pretty much all he said.

Finally, a young man named Noah, who had brown tousled hair and wore running shoes, bounced through the door, apologizing for the long wait and explaining that he was a social worker in psychiatrics. Psychiatrics. The word alarmed me, reminding me of *One Flew Over the Cuckoo's Nest.* Immediately, however, I liked Noah.

"Hey, buddy," he said to Quinn. "Can you tell me what's going on?"

Quinn reddened and managed to get out the words, "I'm just not … happy." This was going to be like pulling teeth, I thought. Quinn hated discussing what was happening to him, even to us.

Noah turned to me instead and I explained what he needed to hear. At one point he asked Quinn if he heard voices. Quinn shook his head. I realized Noah was trying to differentiate between Quinn hearing voices and an OCD bully demanding he do the compulsions. Somehow, Noah got Quinn talking more and they established a rapport, mostly about mountain biking. It didn't take long for Noah, and the doctor who came in later, to ascertain that Quinn was experiencing chronic OCD and needed help immediately. Even though this hospital was in Ontario, Noah got the ball rolling for us on the Quebec side so we'd be bumped up on that two-year waiting list. The goal was to get him to see an OCD children's specialist at a psychiatric hospital in Quebec.

I should mention here that from the friends I'd told about our situation so far — who were steadfast in helping us however they could, researching OCD themselves, and sending me links — one thing kept coming up. People were asking if Quinn's OCD could be a condition called PANDAS, which is OCD brought on by a strep infection. I'd looked into this early on but Quinn didn't fit the profile. In kids with PANDAS, OCD almost always comes on full-blown overnight. Quinn's OCD had come on gradually, triggered over the months from the emotional trauma of losing his grandpa. Still, I asked Noah if we could test Quinn's blood for strep, just in case. They tested him that day. Since I never heard back, I can only assume he tested negative.

When we left the children's hospital, the sun was setting ruby red over the Ottawa horizon. Quinn spent half an hour getting back to the car, a ten-minute walk away. He had to keep stopping to stare up at the sky, hand on heart, and repeat his new chant about winning the hundred-metre race in the 2024 Olympics. He also kept picking up leaves to clutch them and walking backward because he'd "made a mistake" somehow. He got really distressed at one point when a stick he saw on the ground wasn't lying right. Later, he said that the whole walk had been a five on the anxiety scale, that being in new places was torture because there was so much stuff on the ground. By stuff I think he meant leaves and sticks.

Watching my son struggle on the street like that — mumbling to himself as he talked up at the sky, walking backward entire blocks — frightened me to the core. It felt like we were trudging across a bleak tundra rather than through an Ottawa neighbourhood. For the first time I wondered if he'd have to be institutionalized. I was aghast that something that looked like madness could descend like a cyclone out of nowhere into a bright little boy's life.

Quinn, you were skipping along through your childhood so sweetly. Like one of your coloured pencil drawings you were always adding more colour and cars and trees to. Why did you stop?

That night at bedtime, I overheard Quinn telling Rob that he had to tap my dad's picture thirty-six times to win the Olympics. Quinn was kneeling on the dresser, ready to start tapping.

"Thirty-six times? Where did that number come from?" asked Rob. "Why don't you try bargaining with your OCD like we bargained in Mexico? Tell the bully, 'Thirty-six times? Are you kidding me? How about five times?'"

Quinn actually laughed a little. Rob continued. "And then OCD comes back and says, 'What? That's insulting! Thirty times, final offer!' And then, Quinn, you say to the OCD, 'The guy down the street is telling me only five times. Give me a break here, dude, or I'm walking.'" Rob stomped across the bedroom as if on his way to another OCD bully with a better offer. "And then OCD calls you back and says, 'Okay, okay, how about ten times? We have a deal my friend? Ten times? Let's shake.'"

Quinn's face brightened. "Okay, wait, let me try that." He closed his eyes for a few seconds and when he opened them, he said, "Okay, I made a deal. Eight times." He proceeded to tap the picture eight times. When he jumped off the dresser he looked almost triumphant.

I gave a silent thanks to the chance that had brought Rob my way fourteen years before.

Later that night I was in the living room reading yet another book about OCD — the only kind of book I ever read anymore — when Rob came in. I asked him how he did it, how he could stay so positive in the face of losing Quinn. "Doesn't this whole thing depress the hell out of you?"

"Of course it does, but so what? That's a small price to pay. Staying positive is the only option. Nothing else matters. Nothing else matters except...." He stopped talking and sat down on the couch. He closed his eyes. This was the first sign I'd seen of a breakdown in Rob since all this had begun.

"Except what?"

He opened his eyes again. They were wet. "Getting him back."

CHAPTER 20

"Let's just go over your questionnaire again," said the hypnotherapist. She and I were sitting at her kitchen table while Quinn was by himself in the living room. "So, Rob lost his mother when he was eight?" she asked, reading my questionnaire.

"What? No. God, no. His mother lost *her* mother when she was eight. In the 1930s."

"Oh, sorry, I see." She looked down at my questionnaire again. It was obvious she hadn't read it until now.

I was getting impatient with this nonsense. I'd liked what she'd done before with the coloured feet and was hoping she'd do something like that again. "But what does that have to do with Quinn's OCD? OCD is genetic and, in his case, it was triggered by my dad's death."

"Actually, it has everything to do with it. Emotional trauma from his paternal grandmother could be the reason he's going through this today. This might be the key right here." She was pointing at the questionnaire excitedly. "Rob's mother losing her own mother, I really think we have something here." She looked at me intently, her eyes reminding me of a faraway glassy lake.

She then quizzed me about my own mother and how her mother had developed Alzheimer's (although in the 1940s it wasn't called Alzheimer's but a hardening of the arteries leading to the brain) when my mother was sixteen. "So, in effect," said the hypnotherapist, "your mother lost *her* mother when she was young, even though her mother didn't die right away.

And that's similar to Rob's mother losing her mother when she was young."
When she read the part of my questionnaire where I discussed Quinn's birth
she nearly hyperventilated. "Oh, my, this is making so much sense," she said.
"Since Quinn was delivered by an emergency C-section he developed colic."

"Pardon?" I interrupted. "There's no evidence that C-sections cause
colic. I never read about that connection. Colic is something to do with the
nervous system not being fully developed."

She continued reading, ignoring me. "And he was taken away from you
right after the birth. He didn't get to bond with you immediately. This, com-
bined with both his grandmothers losing their mothers. Interesting. This is
all telling me something: He has a bonding anxiety issue." She slapped her
pen down on the table as if that sealed the matter.

Whatever concessions I was willing to make for her flakiness before
had drained away to feeling sheer annoyance. Later in the conversation, she
seemed flummoxed that Quinn's OCD had become stronger, not weaker,
since he'd resolved the grandpa issue. Resolving the grandpa issue up in the
pine tree was something she'd taken full credit for. I told her I'd been reading
about how common it is for OCD to switch themes but that didn't interest
her. She also seemed baffled that Quinn's childhood had been happy until
now, and that he came from a loving family. What puzzled her most of all
was the lack of known murders and suicides in the lives of his ancestors.

"Anyway, I think you'll see a huge improvement when I'm finished with
him today. Hypnosis cures OCD with a ninety-three percent success rate,"
she stated flatly.

"That's incredible," I said. "I find it hard to believe, though. I can't find
anything at all about that online."

"You can't trust the internet," she said.

"Can I ask where you got that statistic? I'm just curious so I can find
it myself."

She thought for a moment and said, "The American ..." and then trailed
off, adding that it was from a real scientific study. When I asked her again
why everyone with OCD wasn't running to the nearest hypnotist if it was so
wildly successful, she said, "Because it's not mainstream."

I sighed. I realized this was probably another $125 down the drain. *But
it's my own fault for being here with this crackpot lady. Maybe I should just run
into the living room right now, grab Quinn, and we can flee out of here.*

Instead, I waited in her kitchen drinking peppermint tea while she and Quinn had their session. At the very least she'll put him in a relaxed state, I thought, give him a forty-five minute vacation from OCD. Half an hour later, they emerged, she leading the way. An unnaturally large smile was stretching her face open. It was hard to tell what was going on with Quinn. He definitely seemed perkier than when we'd arrived, but he also seemed to be trying to tell me something, like, *That was stupid.*

As he was tying his shoelaces to leave I noticed his fists were clenched into balls, which made tying his laces extremely awkward. I couldn't help myself and blurted out, "Oh, Quinn, sweetie, you're still clenching your fists." I was on the verge of tears. I'd just handed over my cash to this woman who was so strongly convinced she'd just helped him and here he was doing one of his most intensely debilitating OCD rituals. And just five minutes after their session had ended.

Back in the car, Quinn immediately said, "That did nothing. She kept talking about family secrets. I didn't know what she was talking about."

A wave of outrage swelled through me. "Family secrets? Like Rob's mother losing her mother in the 1930s, or my grandmother having Alzheimer's? How are those secrets? Anyway, let's not worry about it. Some people are just plain wacky, Quinn. At least we tried."

Still, I was silently steaming as we rolled out of her driveway. Family secrets? What was she thinking saying that to a child? We drove to a nearby pharmacy at a mall. I'd promised Quinn I'd buy him a toy car for having to go through this hellish week of appointments — besides the children's hospital and the hypnotist we were also seeing our family doctor the next day and a private psychologist in Ottawa the day after that.

Like many pharmacies, this one had a turnstile to enter and a different turnstile to exit. After I paid the cashier and had walked back out into the mall, I noticed Quinn was still inside. Over the displays of shampoo I called to him. "Are you coming? Let's go get some lunch somewhere."

He was just standing there, inside the pharmacy. He shook his head. I immediately realized what was happening. He couldn't exit the way he'd entered. The turnstile only goes one way and he was stuck. Suddenly, I was fuming, not at Quinn, of course, but at the hypnotist. Or maybe the person I was most angry at was myself for dragging poor Quinn to see someone like that. What had I been thinking?

I stalked back into the pharmacy and bent down to level my eyes on his. "Quinn, my love, this isn't your fault. I'm going to get you out of here and then we're going back to have a talk with her."

Quinn nodded. I did "the yank," as his soccer coach had done, literally dragging him out of there. He didn't seem to mind.

Back at her house, we sat in the car for ten minutes in the driveway. I didn't know if I should go through with confronting her or not. What good would it do? It was Quinn who finally convinced me. "You should try to get your money back. It didn't work at all," he said quietly from the back seat. He's right, I thought. At the very least I'm showing Quinn that I'm not a chickenshit, that I confront people when the situation warrants it. This warrants it. I wouldn't ask for my money back but I wanted to ask her again about those claims of the success rate of hypnotism on OCD.

I rang her doorbell, my heart hammering, my breathing ragged. When she opened the door I watched a glimmer of unease pass over her face like a dark cloud passing over the sun. It must have been a shock to see me in that state. "I just wanted you to know," I said, "that Quinn's OCD is as bad as ever. He just got stuck at the pharmacy."

She didn't flinch or smile. "Well, it can't be expected to work right away. My kind of work takes patience."

"That's not what you led me to believe. Have you really cured people with OCD as many times as you claimed? And where did you get those statistics?" For some reason that part bothered me more than anything, her quoting me the success rate of hypnotism for OCD.

Again she said she couldn't remember but it had been a real scientific study. I'd find out later it was completely bogus.

That evening I got to thinking about family secrets, not Alzheimer's, but real ones. I'd tried to tell the hypnotist this story but, strangely, she was much more interested in the histories of Quinn's grandmothers. This was a story about my father's father. A few years before my dad died he discovered something surprising about his father. He'd always known that my grandfather had run away from his home in rural Prince Edward Island when he was eleven, and at age twelve he walked the length of Nova Scotia, sleeping in barns and working odd jobs on the way. As twelve-year-olds tend to do. At least in the 1880s. As a young man, he ended up in Maine, perhaps became a communist in Boston, and didn't return to Canada until the outbreak of World War I. He wanted to fight in the war and the only way to do this was to go back to Canada. (The United States wouldn't join the war until 1917.)

By strange circumstance, my dad recently came across his father's World War I record of attestation and enlistment. The document stated that his father, William Gough, was married at the time he joined the Canadian regiment. Married to a woman named Edith Gough. Who was Edith Gough? My dad had no idea. As far as my dad knew, when the war ended his unmarried father left Europe for Montreal. In Montreal, he met a shy, auburn-haired librarian named Jean McDonald, my grandmother. When he met Jean McDonald he didn't tell her he'd been married before, or perhaps, was still married. All those years after running away from home and joining the Canadian army are a mystery. So what became of Edith? Did she die of the Spanish influenza? Was it a bad marriage? Were there children? Did my grandfather simply abandon her? He never once mentioned Edith to my grandmother or to his sons, Patrick and Billy, the boys who loved baseball and birds and whose ashes now lie together at the base of a tree near the Humber River. Apparently my grandfather had secrets that my dad and his brother, Bill, my eccentric historian uncle, could never guess at.

I wondered if it was possible, after all, that family secrets might be lingering somewhere in Quinn's genes. Then again, who comes from a family that doesn't carry old secrets that meander darkly through the bloodstream?

CHAPTER 21

I had no idea how precarious happiness is. Or health. At any moment the wind can gust up and blow these things away from you. I feel like this is all a bad dream or masterminded by an evil warlock and any time now I'll wake up and the nightmare or spell cast on us will be over. Is the world getting darker or has it always been this dire? In the news they keep discussing a terrorist group called the Islamic State of Iraq and the Levant that's slaughtering villagers by the hundreds. The Syrian civil war is raging on and people in the refugee camps are eating dogs and cats to survive. In the United States they've had some debt ceiling crisis that might mean a total collapse of the economy. Every time you read the news there's talk of another superstorm. What once seemed solid and reliable to me as a kid — the world, the future — now feels like a drunken out-of-control brawl. The cumulative weight of all of these new threats is staggering.

Meanwhile, at our house, all Quinn said today was his chant about winning the Olympics. He must have said it several thousand times. His brain has been hijacked by the OCD monster.

I remember something I once read by Garrison Keillor, that even though children may not seem to notice us and they seldom offer us thanks, what we do for them is never, ever, wasted.

I tried to remember this tonight while Quinn was lying next to me at bedtime, stiffened and immobilized with his OCD, seeming not to even know I was there. I decided I'd just talk, tell him stories. I talked for over an hour about our two winters living in San Miguel de Allende, how Quinn used to go out to buy us avocados and limes from the little market around the corner, how the Mexican ladies would sometimes give him a free guava, how Rob once ordered a dozen Thursdays instead of a dozen eggs from those ladies, and the time the school bus driver forgot to stop at the bus stop on the way home, just kept barrelling down the highway with Quinn inside and I had to flag a taxi and chase the bus. I talked about how when we went to the dental hygienist's house to get our teeth cleaned for twenty-five dollars her little dog would sit on our laps as she polished our stains away, and about the time when Quinn's grade one teacher gave Quinn the starring role as Joseph in a nativity play but didn't tell him he was playing Joseph until he was onstage in front of the audience. As Rob and I sat and watched, Quinn held the hand of a little Mexican girl playing Mary and we could see how bewildered he was.

I'm pretty sure my words got through to Quinn because he let out a tiny snigger at that last story.

Sometimes you have to look for just one or two good things in an otherwise lousy situation, just to set yourself at ease for a while. On James Bay, in the midst of my time teaching there, I'd sometimes escape that wretched abuse-ridden village and walk to a nearby frozen bog with some little girls in my class — the few who weren't tragically violent and unreachable — and we'd giggle as we did cartwheels in the snow and I told them about Anne of Green Gables and they told me about goose camp. Many nights on James Bay, after a teaching day unleashed from hell, I'd step outside my little house into the lung-splitting Arctic air and look skyward to watch the aurora borealis cha-cha a green shimmering swath across the sky like Fred Astaire cutting up a rug. I'd let the whole celestial carnival sink inside me until I felt better.

I have to find something positive about each day or I'll become completely unhinged. This is what I found today:

1) Our family doctor saw Quinn again this morning and realized, like Noah at the children's hospital, that Quinn must be red flagged asap to see the child OCD specialist at the psychiatric hospital.

2) Quinn is now making himself write, "I will win the 2024 Olympics ..." over and over. I told him that if he was going to write that he should at least use cursive rather than printing. (For the past few years I've been showing him cursive since, incredibly, they no longer teach cursive at his school.) Then he wrote the phrase about the Olympics, beautifully, eighteen times.

3) I had a break last night and went over to where Chantal is staying and it was like a vacation back to the old me. She found what I was telling her so strange and unreal that she laughed hysterically. Again! Just like at the restaurant! For some reason I find it a huge relief to see her react this way. I have no idea why. The sheer absurdity of life maybe? We're all actors in a surreal play? In any case, visiting Chantal helped nudge some clouds out of the way, at least for a while.

4) Mum advised me to forget the "hypnotist charlatan" and not to put any more energy into it. She's right. As of now I've completely let it go. Peace and good fortune to you, flaky lady!

We were lucky to get a call from a private psychologist who had a cancellation that week. On Friday morning, it was raining and the three of us drove to Dr. Cebulski's office in Westboro, an Ottawa neighbourhood full of fair trade cafés, young families, and sporting equipment stores. Quinn took forever getting up the stairs of the office building, backtracking and erasing his steps. Finally, we were all seated in the doctor's office on cushy chairs, facing each other. The office felt like a living room, with a softly lit lamp, paintings of canoes on lakes, and a window view of shoppers scurrying along sidewalks beneath umbrellas. Dr. Cebulski seemed like the kind of person you'd like as a neighbour, quiet-spoken, friendly, and full of stories. We explained to him how Quinn's obsession had switched from wanting my dad back to winning the Olympics, that Quinn was squeezing his fists tight most of the day, chanting, backtracking, and performing countless other rituals all in the hopes of winning the hundred-metre race in 2024.

"Oh, that's like baseball players!" said Dr. Cebulski. Immediately, I liked him even more.

"So, Quinn," he said, "you know how when the batters get up to bat a lot of them start touching the rims of their helmet a certain number of times, or unstrapping and restrapping their gloves, or toe-tapping after each swing, or crossing themselves, or holding their bats up high in the air?" Quinn nodded. "Some of them take the exact same route each time to get to the batter's box. One guy draws an intricate symbol into the dirt with his bat every time. There are all kinds of things these guys do in that batter's box. Do you know why they do those things?"

"To get a hit?" said Quinn in a near-whisper.

"That's right. To get a hit. Do you think doing those funny things helps them get a hit?"

Quinn shook his head.

"I don't, either. The guys who do those things and the guys who don't do them all have a batting average of around three hundred, which means seven out of ten times they don't get on base."

I liked Dr. Cebulski's laid-back, subtle approach. His words seemed like they'd sink in. I felt badly that Quinn was so clamped up, hardly uttering a word when Dr. Cebulski asked him questions. We'd decided beforehand that the last half-hour of the appointment would be just Rob and me learning what we could from Dr. Cebulski while Quinn sat in the waiting room. When Quinn's half-hour was up, he shot out of the office like a mouse from a trap. He hated being the centre of attention at the best of times. Dr. Cebulski told us we were doing all the right things with the cognitive behaviour therapy, mentioning we could concentrate on the cognitive part even more, as in getting behind the logic of winning a race at the Olympics. "Ask him what will happen if he doesn't win the Olympics. Get him to explain the connection between closing his fists and saying his chant and how that could affect his chance of winning a race eleven years from now. Ask him what would happen if he opens his hands up today. Does he really think that could make him lose a race when he's twenty-one years old?"

I kept nodding my head. I liked hearing this because we'd been doing it all along. I just hadn't thought it could work because it was too logical and OCD seemed everything *but* logical.

Dr. Cebulski then said something so chilling that I felt a cold ripple snake up my spine. In his soft-spoken voice he said, "You two are in for a long ride. Quinn seems to have full-blown OCD."

I stared back at him. I guess I'd realized this but hated hearing it confirmed by someone who'd obviously seen a lot of cases. He continued, saying, "Maybe when Quinn is fifteen or sixteen he'll start figuring this all out, start learning how to manage it."

I felt the bottom fall out of my stomach. Fifteen or sixteen? I sat there speechless in the chasm of his statement. We'd now *officially* been thrown from the path of our lives. Hurled. Catapulted. Sky-rocketed.

After the appointment, we drove to nearby Chinatown to pick up some greens at a Chinese grocer and get some lunch. As we walked along Somerset Street, Quinn kept falling behind to stop and put his hand on his heart, chant his Olympics mantra, and, often, hop backward. I couldn't help noticing that people strolling by on the busy street were witnessing this, probably assuming he was a boy in serious trouble, which, I suppose, he was. It was the first time he'd actually performed this many visible all-consuming rituals with so many people around. In the hospital neighbourhood earlier in the week, the suburban streets had been nearly deserted. As I watched Quinn shuffle and murmur his way through Chinatown I tried to see him through the eyes of strangers. I only did this for a second though because I thought my heart might crack in two.

At the Pho Bo Ga Restaurant we ordered large steaming bowls of vegetable noodle soup. "Hey, Quinn," said Rob. "I have an idea. Think of something you really want. Not to win the Olympics but something else." Just then the waiter brought Quinn his mango shake. Rob moved it to the other side of the table, out of Quinn's reach. "Okay, you want this shake, right? What's something you can do to make it come to you?"

"Ask for it, saying please?" said Quinn.

"What else?" said Rob. "How about clapping your hands four times and humming a tune? Will that make the shake magically slide over to you?" Quinn shook his head. Later, after we'd eaten and were waiting for the bill, Rob said, "Hey, I'd rather not pay our bill. Quinn, do you think if I put on my hat and make this funny face and chant the words, *I won't pay my bill, I won't pay my bill*, that we'll still have to pay our bill?" Quinn's eyes had become very big. He was transfixed. "Watch this," continued Rob. Rob put on his hat, made a Mr. Bean face and starting chanting in a frog voice that he didn't want the bill to come. I joined him with an Ethel Merman voice. Then Quinn started chanting in a silly voice, too. We were sitting in a crowded Vietnamese restaurant chanting in frog, Oompa Loompa, and Ethel Merman voices, "We don't want our bill to come, we don't want our bill to come." Customers eating nearby stopped talking to stare, looking curiously amused.

The bill came anyway. "I guess our magical thinking didn't work that time," said Rob. "Oh, well, maybe next time."

CHAPTER 22

JOURNAL

We've been going full throttle with the cognitive behaviour therapy. This afternoon I got Quinn to read aloud because we've discovered that if he reads aloud without pausing he can go three or four minutes without having to chant. During a timed ten minutes when he was trying not to read everything that he'd read me backward, we watched some Olympics races on my tablet. We watched Usain Bolt, the Jamaican sprinter, and a bunch of Kenyans. "Do you see a pattern here?" I asked Quinn. "These guys winning the hundred-metre races are all big, tall, and black. You're not. What do you think your chances are?" The colour drained from Quinn's face. Clearly devastated, he started chanting repeatedly.

The next night at dinner Rob tried another ERP experiment. Only this time he tried it on me. He moved the tablecloth so it was all bunched and crooked. He also moved all our placemats so they were off-kilter and folded over. He winked at Quinn, turned to me, and said, "So, I bet you'd love to set this stuff back the way it goes, right?" It was true. It was driving me crazy how askew everything was. Maybe this was OCD. I'd never thought of it that way before. I recalled how as a kid I'd liked all the ornaments on my bedroom dresser to be perfectly arranged. And my dad liked all his books and papers to be at ninety-degree angles on his desk. I guess these things are a tinge OCD. Rob asked if it was bugging me to see the table messed up like that and I said it was bugging me a lot. "How do you feel on a scale of one to five?" he asked. I said maybe a three. Quinn moved his glass of water to the extreme edge of the table, something he knows drives me to distraction. He and Rob exchanged conspiratorial glances. Rob started timing me to see how long I could go without having to move everything back to where it belonged.

"Whoa, this isn't easy! I don't like this one bit," I said, looking at the things awry and the water about to crash to the floor. "Quinn, I can see how hard this must be to hold back, to not do what you feel like doing. This is awful!"

"I know!" said Quinn.

That evening I went to the community centre to watch an all-candidates debate for an upcoming local election. When it was over I saw my friend Isabel in the parking lot. Sometimes all it takes for a torrent of emotion to come pouring out is a good friend giving you a worried look and asking you how you are. I couldn't even answer her. I just broke down sobbing. She hugged me and then I cried and howled all the way home in my car.

When I got back I could see that Quinn had been crying, too. He told me how unfair it was that all the guys who win those races are tall and black. I explained to him, not for the first time, that until 1904 black people weren't even allowed to compete in the Olympics at all and how unfair was that? "I know this is your OCD doing this to you, giving you these obsessions that don't make sense and making you do these rituals. Isn't OCD a nasty evil bully?"

He stared at me. The silence filling the space between us felt unnerving and then I realized it was because he wasn't chanting. Suddenly, his face flooded with hot tears as he stood bereft in front of me. He collapsed to the floor pounding his clenched fists on the rug and shrieked, "My dream is dead! My dream is dead! I'll never win!"

A tsunami of alarm swirled through me. His grief looked as severe as it had been over my dad dying. This is OCD, I kept telling myself. *And if this Olympics obsession is receding, what in God's name will the next one be?* He ran to his room and flung himself on his bed, where he lay with his eyes closed, unmoving, unreachable. When I asked him if I could read to him or sing to him or hug him goodnight, instead of shaking his head no, he flitted his closed eyes back and forth so he wouldn't have to move his head.

We'd lost him again.

That night as Rob and I lay in bed, the waning moonlight flowing through our window, Rob said, "I don't think we can do this alone any more. Except for Tina, Anna, and your mother, it feels like we've isolated ourselves."

I looked out the window at the trees blowing in the autumn wind. I heard squirrels scurrying around in our attic, trying to move in for the winter. "It doesn't have to be this way," I said. "We have so many friends. Wakefield is such an amazing community. We can start telling more people. They'll help us. Even if people just came by to ask how it's going. At least you and I could get out for a walk." I paused, wondering if we'd meant for this whole thing to be a secret. I realized we hadn't. It had just become that way on its own. "Let's tell everybody."

That one small decision made me feel like I'd just turned my face toward the sun on a spring day. *We won't be alone any more.* Wakefield, somehow, could help us. I thought of how often I'd felt lucky to live in Wakefield. Sometimes walking home late at night beside the river, after hearing music at the Black Sheep or at the open stage at the local pub, I'd stop to watch the moon wandering across the sky above the water. I'd stand there letting that bright moon gallop me back over the years to recall that I'd always dreamed of living in a place like this: where the wild woods you tramp through sustain you to your very core, where you can dive deep into a cool river at midnight when you're hot, and, best of all, where everyone you pass on the street smiles and says hi. *I'm so lucky to live here*, I always think, *so lucky that after all my traipsing around this place found me.*

We won't be alone any more. It was that singular thought that let me sleep that night.

CHAPTER 23

I woke up too early the next morning. Out in the garden I heard chickadees, their normally jokey chirping now sounding a little shrill. I was trying to lie still so I wouldn't wake Quinn downstairs. His OCD meant it took him hours to fall asleep at night, and he was constantly exhausted. But then I heard a shuffling noise and saw that Quinn had crawled into bed beside Rob. I went over to cuddle him while he slept, wondering what would happen now that his Olympics dream had died. I remembered it was Saturday. I ventured to say, "Hey, I want to buy carrots from the Czechoslovakian goat herder at the Tailgate Market this morning. Then we should go to Chamberlain's Lookout for breakfast!"

To both my and Rob's amazement, Quinn pumped his fist in the air. "Yes!" he said, still with his eyes closed, smiling.

"Are you going to order the Little Lad Special?" I asked, barely believing what was happening.

Quinn didn't reply. He still had his eyes shut, half-asleep. I started tickling him. Then Rob began tickling him, too. Quinn started giggling. I hadn't heard this kind of giggling come out of Quinn in a long time. *Had he dropped his obsession? Was he back to normal?* As the tickling continued the giggling started subsiding. Gradually, a look of unease began to cross his face as his brow wrinkled. Then his body stiffened. No more giggling. I asked him again what he was going to order for breakfast, even though I could see we probably wouldn't be going after all. With his eyes still shut, he shook his head, his expression contorting like he was holding back a great tide of pain, the torment clearly etched all over his face. It was as if the OCD monster was just now waking up, getting ready to take over again. Before that, for a few precious moments, we'd had the old giggly Quinn with us. Now that boy was gone again.

It was probably the single saddest moment of my life.

I couldn't help myself. Tears stung my eyes. I ran downstairs and rushed outside in my pyjamas, my bare feet slapping the cold smooth rock of the pathway to our house. I fled to the car. I got inside and closed the door. Great heaving sobs started to shake my body. The world felt dangerously futile, like a chasm was opening in the ground and I might plummet head-first and never stop falling. Between gulps of crying I started pleading, "I just want my boy back. I just want my boy back." And also, *We need help.* I howled those words over and over. I repeated them so many times and sobbed so much that after a while, I had nothing left inside me.

I tried to pull myself together but after breakfast I found myself fighting tears again as I washed the dishes. I looked over at the dining room table, at Rob trying to get Quinn to do some exposure exercises that involved drawing. Quinn looked like a pale ghost, completely shut down. I burst out crying. It happened so fast that it actually scared me. Rob immediately got up and told Quinn they should go upstairs. Ten minutes later Rob came down again. I was still in the kitchen, still choking back tears, searching for some frozen bananas in the freezer. Rob closed the freezer door and fixed his gaze on me. His face reminded me of cement, hard and devoid of colour. I'd never seen him look like that. "I can't help you," he said at last, his exhausted, glazed eyes full of red. "I have no energy for anything but Quinn."

I swallowed. "It's okay. I don't expect anything. I *want* you to put all your energy into Quinn. I understand." My voice sounded like it had escaped from a rusty tin can. I tried to smile as I reached for his arm. Both of us seemed to be stumbling around lately on short staggered breaths. It felt like we were in some kind of war, battling it out in muddy soul-decaying trenches. *We need some air,* I thought, *a Christmas truce, a friendly soccer game against the OCD monster. Couldn't we make friends with the enemy, even just for a day?*

That afternoon Rob left to operate the sound and video at a memorial for a fourteen-year-old girl named India. This girl had recently died of an extremely rare genetic disease in which at the end of her life she was having seizures every five seconds. Although she lived near Wakefield, nobody I knew had ever met her since her condition kept her inside. As Quinn and I worked on some of his exposure exercises, I kept thinking of the girl's parents. I couldn't begin to imagine what they were going through. When Rob came home he said that India's memorial had been beautiful. His eyes looked almost shiny, his pupils dilated. Somehow the death of this young girl he'd never met had deeply moved him.

"Just imagine, in all those months when her parents knew she was going to die, imagine if they'd been told there was a slight chance she could keep living but she'd have severe OCD all her life. Imagine how they'd lunge at that chance like it was a miracle, how lucky they'd feel. We still have Quinn and he has severe OCD. He's in there and we can help him find his way out. But even if we don't, we still have him."

We stared at each other. He was right. I thought of the parents who'd rushed their kid with the broken arm into the hospital, how lucky I'd thought they were. I tried to muster up some of Rob's mindset. All I could think of were the girl's parents. If I was dangling on the edge of hopelessness, how must they be feeling?

I still wanted to reach out to people as I'd resolved the night before but I found myself so depleted that I could barely get off the couch. Sleep deprived and with a throbbing head from so much crying, all I wanted was for this hell to be over. Outside, I could hear crows cawing and, in the distance, the sound of kids playing down the road.

A meteorite. Why couldn't a meteorite hit our house and let this miserable new life of ours be finished within a flash?

Should I put something on Facebook? I wondered. Should I tell people about our situation that way? At that moment I thought it should be renamed Fakebook. If you wonder how your own life is going you just go to Fakebook to find out. *Oh, good, I look so happy in these photos. I'm having so much fun. My life must be fantastic!* I decided against using Facebook to tell people about Quinn.

That night we had to cancel our plans to go to Anna's house for a spaghetti dinner. There was no way Quinn could manage it. Instead, we made spaghetti ourselves at home. After dinner, Quinn ran up and down the stairs twenty-two times in eleven minutes. "Is that an OCD thing? Training for the Olympics or something?" I asked Rob. "Yep," he said, not looking up from his book. "But at least he's getting some exercise."

EMAIL, SUNDAY, OCTOBER 27, 2013

To our friends,

I'm not sure how many of you know that Quinn has developed severe OCD (obsessive compulsive disorder). It started out mildly in the spring but, disturbingly, has been ramping up in the last couple of months. It's a neurological disorder and in Quinn's case it's extreme and getting more so by the day. He has stopped going to school and can no longer live a single OCD-free moment during his waking day. Rob (who is proving to be much stronger than I am in this, absolutely a rock of determination) mentioned the other night that we're alone in this thing, maybe because we don't want to scare people. It's pretty freaky to see someone who such a short time ago was a happy-go-lucky, bike-riding kid now barely able to walk down the road or even talk. So I'm telling you this because we need help and I don't even know what kind of help. If people could visit once in a while that would go a long way in lifting our spirits. Rather than try to explain it, I'm going to insert the note I just wrote about his morning today.

"Quinn is still lying in bed at 10 a.m. I open the curtains and climb up the ladder of his bunk bed to see him. His eyes are shut but I can tell he's awake. He's immobile. I move a teddy bear out of the way and he makes a distressed noise. I put it back exactly where it was. I try to get him talking, ask what he'd like for breakfast. No answer, no movement. Finally, he says quietly, in a robot voice, "Close curtain. Curtain close." (If he says the words backward it erases it.) All I can do is close the curtain and walk out of the room. Rob gives it a try and comes out telling me he thinks Quinn just needs to wake up on his own time now. Ten minutes later, Quinn emerges and throws himself down crouched on the living room floor. When I try to hug him he backs away looking terrified. "What?" I say. "I can't even hug you now?" He shakes his head. I poke his toe and say jokingly, "Can I touch your toe?" He yells, "No! Touch again. Again touch." So now I have to touch his toe to "erase" what I did. Only it turns out that I don't touch it in exactly the right place that I touched it before so he panics and does this high-pitched distress call until I find the right place on his toe. "So I can't even hug my own son?" I say. Rob tells me I can't react emotionally or it will make it worse. I feel like running outside and shouting HELP US to the world. But what can anyone do? Saddest of all, he's supposed to be at a pumpkin carving party down the street right now. The real Quinn was excited about it and of course wanted to go. But the OCD monster inside his head would never allow something like that. And forget about Halloween. What will we do Halloween night? There's no way he can go out trick-or-treating and he'd never want the kids to see him if they came here."

We know that the real Quinn is still in there somewhere. We get to see him sometimes. But I would give anything in the entire world to get my son back for good.

So now you know why you haven't seen Quinn or even us around. But if you'd like to drop by, we would love it. We need our friends and we need Quinn back. There is nothing more important to us in the entire universe than getting our son back to the happy kid we used to know.

Love,
Laurie

P.S. Feel free to forward this since I'm so tired I'm probably forgetting a bunch of people. BTW, the attached photo was taken by a passing photographer in Guelph in June. When I look at it now I see he's doing an OCD thing (touching his dead grandpa's watch — his grandpa dying is what triggered this whole thing). At the time, we had no idea touching the watch meant anything and just thought it was nice how much he liked the watch as a way to remember his grandpa.

If only it had all stopped with touching the watch.

CHAPTER 24

After writing that letter, everything changed.

The phone began ringing almost immediately. Emails flooded my inbox. An astounding outpouring of love and support began to flow into our lives from friends, neighbours, and the larger Wakefield community. My neighbour Christine from down the street, the mother of two of Quinn's oldest friends, was completely shocked and distressed. She said she had no idea any of this was happening. She told me she'd do anything at all to help us, including talking to the school principal. Another neighbour, a naturopath, told me she'd help me with remedies. My friend Stephanie in British Columbia who is a doctor called to say I should call her whenever I couldn't sleep, even if it was 3 a.m. Emails came from all over. People I didn't even know began writing to me, friends of friends who had experience with OCD. There was even talk of raising money for us with a local art auction, which we declined, but it was a lovely gesture.

I realized I should have written that letter much sooner.

Tina's email was especially insightful:

> Dear Laurie,
>
> Please don't be mad at me for saying this, but absolutely do not help Quinn with his OCD rituals. Helping him confirms that the OCD is in charge and should be obeyed. I know it's really

hard to see him freak out like you described in your letter but you must not enable the OCD. It's normal for a parent to help a kid get over his anxieties like that, so your reaction is totally understandable, but people with OCD shouldn't be handled that way. It will aggravate the behaviour. Do you remember how strong and matter-of-fact your mother was when she spoke to him? How brutally honest? And how well it worked? He needs that kind of strength. That kind of head-on fierceness. There's no wincing in the face of OCD. It can smell fear. I'm really sorry that I didn't tell you sooner. I thought you knew already. I know you've done a ton of research. I have total faith in you and Rob. I know you guys will make the right decisions. It's going to be really hard, on everyone, but I know you guys can get through it. And maybe one day your story will help others, too. Let me know if there's anything else I can do.

I love you!

Take care of yourself too! Ganbatte!!!

Tina

I knew Tina was right about not kowtowing to Quinn's OCD bully. With his OCD so much worse lately, I'd been wearing down, often too beat to fight the bully myself. But now I had a new resolve. Writing that letter felt like I'd released this secret of ours out into the world, freeing it from our sad little home of three. Now our secret had wings and was flying through the community at lightning speed. A lot more friends knew and somehow that made everything feel easier.

Also, I didn't realize it at the time, but writing that letter was a tipping point. Before the letter, we had no idea how far down Quinn would go. Would he end up like the kids we'd seen on videos of a place called Extreme OCD Camp? Would he have to be institutionalized? But after that letter, somehow everything felt lighter in our house. The scales had tipped in our favour. Even if all people did was send a simple two-line email saying they were thinking of us and sending us love, it made a difference. I'm not sure how this worked but somehow I thought it would ultimately make a difference to Quinn, too. Perhaps it was the ripple effect. The best part was something I hadn't even anticipated. People started coming by and, as it turns out, the OCD monster hates visitors.

The very next afternoon, our neighbour Christine sent her son Liam over to play with Quinn. Liam was two years younger than Quinn and the two of them had been friends since Liam was a toddler and just learning to talk. Liam was always talking. And smiling. In fact, I'd never seen another human smile so much in my life. He never failed to brighten my day when he came to our door. When he came over that afternoon he didn't seem to care at all that Quinn was acting a bit "unusual," as he called it. He was just happy to play with his friend. "Hey, Quinn, that's funny how you're scrunching up your fists like that. Isn't it hard to pick up your cars?" I pretended not to listen as I read a magazine. This was exactly the kind of thing I was hoping Liam would say. Quinn had to loathe his OCD. He had to be embarrassed by it, see how much it interfered with everyday life. Quinn shrugged. "Yeah, kind of hard." He picked up a toy car between his clenched fists and the two of them started laughing. Ten minutes later they were out on the driveway, Quinn on his unicycle, Liam on his bike. I could overhear Liam talking. "I guess it's kind of hard to ride your bike when you can't open your fists, huh, Quinn? Your unicycle is perfect for you! No hands needed!" It was as if I'd been feeding Liam lines. He seemed to have a knack for saying exactly the right thing to someone with OCD. The part that made my heart soar more than anything, though, was that they were having fun. Quinn hadn't had any sustained fun in a very long time. If only I'd invited Liam over here earlier, I thought.

That evening, our friend Brant showed up with a pizza. Quinn and Brant had a special loving relationship that involved stomping on each other's feet. Brant, Quinn, and I were in the kitchen while I tossed a salad. Quinn was drinking a glass of mango juice with his fists clenched. This made holding the glass an unwieldy manoeuvre.

"So, Quinn," said Brant tentatively, his big brown eyes squinting sideways, "I'm kind of wondering, what's with the fists?"

Quinn looked at me, hoping I'd answer for him. I shrugged. "Magic bubbles," said Quinn. Under his breath, he whispered, "bubbles magic." He was becoming adept at erasing his words without people noticing.

"Magic bubbles?" asked Brant. "What are magic bubbles?"

Again, Quinn looked at me, willing me to answer for him. "You tell him," I said.

Quinn inhaled a deep gulp of air, gearing up to say more than a few words at a time. This is exactly what we needed him to do, to act like a normal person again. "I'm holding on to magic bubbles. If I let them go, I won't win the eight-hundred-metre race in the 2024 Olympics." After seeing all those videos of black athletes winning the hundred metres his obsession had switched to the eight hundred metres. Some white guys actually win that one apparently.

Brant tilted his head, thinking about this. "Interesting." He rubbed his goatee. In his slow, thoughtful way of talking, he said, "I've heard a lot of athletes talk about how they got to the Olympics, how they won races. Training, mostly. I don't recall any athletes ever mentioning anything about … magic bubbles."

Brant's words hovered in the air. Nobody said anything. We all seemed to be taking turns looking at each other. I took a sip of wine. Suddenly, Quinn busted out a rip-rattling laugh. He started laughing so hard he doubled over. Brant and I joined him. I couldn't remember when anything had seemed more hilarious. Quinn seemed to think so, too. He just kept cackling with laughter. Later, I'd realize it was one of those openings, a crack in his OCD armour when he caught a glimpse of the absurdity behind it all.

This is what that letter has done, I thought. This is what our friends can do for us, bring some normalcy back to Quinn's life, to our life. Each visit to our house felt like a bright peephole into the world we used to know. I felt something shift in our house the night that Brant visited, like tectonic plates gliding barely perceptibly beneath the surface. Brant suggested to Quinn that he try transferring the magic bubble in his right hand into his left. "That way you at least have a free hand." Quinn tried this. He ate pizza with his free hand. After dinner, I was up in our office for a few moments while Brant and Rob were downstairs playing their guitars. Quinn came in, his face brimming with good news. He held up his open hand to me for a high five. Then he held up the other hand, too. Both his hands were wide open. I couldn't remember how long he'd had those fists clenched. I pulled him in and squeezed him tight, then rushed downstairs to hug Brant goodbye. I don't think Brant could have realized what he'd done for us that night.

I took care of a little girl named Ruby the next day. Ruby had just turned three. It was a part-time job of mine to be a backup caregiver for Ruby and I loved having her at our house. She could easily sit with me for two hours straight as I read her one storybook after the next. She'd listen entranced to the stories of Enid Blyton, Margaret Wise Brown, and Dr. Seuss. We'd make chocolate chip cookies and I'd let her eat chocolate chips and walnuts while the cookies baked. We'd walk in the forest and spend long dreamy moments staring at caterpillars.

She was curious about Quinn, the big boy who she knew lived at the house and until now had always been at school. Ruby's presence forced another human interaction, much like Liam's and Brant's had the day before, in which Quinn's OCD stood out to him like a Goth at a pep rally. Quinn and I were standing in the hallway and Ruby was standing squarely in front of Quinn. He was having some kind of OCD episode where everything had to be a certain way. He didn't like it that she'd moved slightly to the right. So he said to Ruby, "Please move. Move please." Being just newly three, she just stood there staring up at him with her perfectly round blue eyes. He said it again. She kept standing there, staring at him, unmoving. Rob happened to be nearby watching this and said to Quinn, "Maybe Ruby doesn't do OCD." I looked down at her. "Ruby, do you do OCD?" I asked. She shook her head, solemnly gazing up at us as if she knew exactly what we were talking about, and had read the latest in OCD brain research. "No, I don't," she said determinedly. I laughed. And then Quinn did, too. It was the perfect response. Even a three-year-old wouldn't obey the OCD bully.

That week, Rob announced that Quinn's numbers on the Excel chart they used to track his anxiety levels had been going down. Quinn wasn't as panicked about not doing the behaviours as he had been. Something was happening to him.

Still, I was continually struck by what an insatiable monster OCD is. The more you give in, the hungrier it gets. Even Howard Hughes with all his millions couldn't buy his way out of an OCD stranglehold, although it's not commonly known. It didn't help that his servants were forever helping him perform the outlandish rituals that his OCD demanded. (As an interesting side note, when Leonardo DiCaprio played Howard Hughes in the movie *Aviator*, the actor stopped trying to control his own OCD during the weeks of filming so he'd do a more authentic job portraying the OCD of the famous millionaire. DiCaprio was often late on the film set because of his compulsion to retrace his footsteps, avoid cracks in the pavement, and need to walk through doorways multiple times. It took him months to get his OCD under control again after filming stopped. And speaking of actors, if

I'd only known at the time, I could have told Quinn that Daniel Radcliffe, the Harry Potter star, had serious OCD as a young child, sometimes taking five minutes to turn off a light switch. "I had to repeat every sentence I said under my breath," said the actor in an interview.)

One evening that week, Rob said to Quinn, "What would you do if a car salesman said you could have a Bugatti Veyron or some other fancy Italian super-car for only ten dollars?"

"I'd say sure!" Quinn clapped his hands at the thought of the car.

"Right. So the guy says, 'Give me the ten dollars and come back tomorrow. You can't have the car today.' So you pay him ten dollars and go back the next day. No car. The guy says, 'Oh, sorry, pay me another ten dollars and I'll give you the car in a couple of days.' So you pay the guy again and come back in a couple of days. Still no car. And again, the guy wants another ten dollars. Every time you go he makes you pay him ten dollars but he never delivers the car. The lying salesman is OCD. Always lying, never delivering. He's selling an impossible dream: to bring Grandpa back, to win an Olympic race eleven years from now. He keeps you hooked, always coming back for more." Rob paused. Quinn was looking at him intently, barely blinking. "What if you just stopped talking to the guy?"

Quinn squinted as if thinking hard about this, then said, "I get it. I know the OCD is lying to me. But that doesn't mean I can stop."

"You can stop," said Rob.

It seemed to me that logic could enter and clear out a space for him to stop for a few moments, but then the compulsions would take over again. This was his primitive "old brain" at work. The old brain, which is evolutionarily older, is often at odds with the new, more evolved, front part of the brain, which is more of a reasoning machine. The old brain wants what it wants when it wants it. The "new brain" tells us to put the brakes on when we feel compelled to do something that the old brain wants to do, but we don't always listen. It reminded me of how sometimes chocolate pops into my head and within seconds I'm eating a hunk of dark sea salt chocolate. I hadn't bothered waiting for the more evolved reasoning part of my brain to stop me. We evolved to crave sugar and fat because they were scarce and needed to be eaten when the opportunity arose. The old brain doesn't know that too much dark sea salt chocolate isn't good for us. But the new brain is fully aware of this. Yet sometimes we just say to hell with the new brain and eat the chocolate anyway, succumb to our old-brain compulsions. The OCD bully was lurking somewhere in Quinn's old brain, slithering through trapdoors and finding hidden passages. Interestingly, the old brain, which is always in survival mode, doesn't know the difference between past and present. It's the part of our brain that acts instinctively when it senses danger, sending fight or flight messages to the new brain. For those with OCD, the old brain is constantly firing off danger signals to the new brain even though danger isn't there. The new brain can see how unreasonable the whole thing is but is overwhelmed with all the warnings. *Quick!* says the old brain, *Say this mantra ten times or you'll never see your grandpa again!* As one man in the Ottawa OCD parent support group that I attended said, "OCD is one part of your brain lying to another part of your brain and that other part of the brain not knowing it's a lie." This man had OCD himself and said something else that tore through me like a cold dagger. He said he believes OCD digs down into your deepest subconscious, finds the darkest thing in there, and then turns that thing against you. I imagined Quinn's OCD bully as a nasty little snivelling octopus-like dictator. I wanted to throttle the thing with a mallet. OCD hunts down the most hidden regions of a person, its suckered tentacles inching along, prowling, and slithering into the most locked box it can find. No matter how unlikely an event (a dead person returning to life, a white kid winning the Olympics by holding magic bubbles in his fists, sudden death by touching a doorknob) if there's even a fraction of a possibility that the event could occur, OCD will find its way to lodge and furl inside you, making promises it can never deliver, ever tightening its death grip.

In *Riveted*, by Jim Davies, the author suggests that if you doubt how your old-brain biases can conflict with what you know intellectually, you should try a certain thought experiment. He asks you to imagine how you'd feel putting on a newly washed shirt that Adolph Hitler had worn. If the thought creeps you out more than imagining wearing a washed shirt of a regular person, you're feeling the power of this effect.

Quinn had somewhat of a setback the next day, during what I'd starting thinking of as the week of Operation Normalization (which came about serendipitously after I'd written the letter and people started coming by). He was slumped on the couch, telling me it was too hard to go out and play with Liam.

"Playing isn't hard. You've been playing all your life. OCD is *making* it hard," I said, exasperated. "Do you really want to spend the next eleven years not having fun and being bossed around by OCD every second of the day just to win some race?"

To my surprise, Quinn bolted up off the chair. "That's true. I think I will play." He stormed over to the closet, threw on his jacket, and was out the door in seconds. I pumped my fist in the air and mouthed a silent *Yes!* at the ceiling.

Half an hour later, Christine called to tell me that she'd been watching out her window and Quinn was hiding by himself in the woods. "And before that he was trying to ride his bike backward. He seems to be having some trouble."

Operation Normalization, like the rest of this journey, seemed to be two steps forward, one step back.

JOURNAL

Today I ran into a woman at the Wakefield General Store who'd seen my letter about Quinn. Someone had forwarded it to her. Like the woman who talked about the "native animal connection," she also talked about "Spirit" telling her things. She was almost breathless, as if she couldn't wait for me to receive this important information. She said, "Spirit told me something and it makes so much sense. I know what needs to happen for your son: third chakra." I said, "What?" She replied, "His third chakra needs to be realigned with his sixth chakra. He'd need a shaman to do this, of course. But I know of one."

I stared at her for a long time to see if she was joking. She didn't seem to be. Finally, I said, "Wow, that sounds really scientific."

She went on trying to explain her theory, in more detail. Normally this would have seemed a riot to me. I would have tested myself to see how long I could keep a straight face.

All I want is for life to return to itself. There's no FUN left. I'm pretty sure we used to have nothing but fun. It was the magic carpet beneath our feet, it spiralled out of the sky, it flew in from Jupiter, it dwelt in our DNA. What happened to it? I don't even have an appetite. I don't even want dark chocolate any more. How can this be? I've lost weight. I don't even care. Normally I might be pleased about this but what does it matter? On top of all this, tomorrow is Halloween. We haven't even bought a pumpkin this year. Or Halloween candy. Every Halloween Rob sets up his shop by the laneway and makes it look scary and builds a campfire and loops that Tom Waits song, "What's He Building?" so the kids hear it over and over. Do we just pretend Halloween isn't happening?

Meanwhile, I'm waiting for hope to settle inside me, the hope that my husband and everyone else seems to be talking about, the hope that's a lifeline to keep people afloat.

CHAPTER 25

I was born on the night of Samhain, when the barrier between the worlds is whisper-thin and when magic, old magic, sings its heady and sweet song to anyone who cares to hear it.

— Carolyn MacCullough, *Once a Witch*

When Quinn woke up on October 31, he announced he wanted to go out for Halloween that night. I was thrilled, but dubious. His fists were back to being clenched, containing the Olympic-winning magic bubbles. He was still backtracking everywhere, still erasing words. I couldn't imagine how he'd put on a costume, let alone walk down the street without getting stuck, or talk to people on their front porches. Nonetheless, I encouraged him. "Have you thought of a costume yet?"

"Ninja fighter. Fighter ninja." I had no idea where this idea had come from but told him it sounded perfect. We could look in the Halloween box for black clothes and a mask and could fashion a sword of some kind.

We'd been lucky to get another appointment with Dr. Cebulski, scheduled for four o'clock that day. The timing wasn't great. We'd have to rush home from Ottawa after the appointment, grab something for dinner, then wait for Quinn to clench-fist a costume on, all in time for him to meet the neighbour kids out on our road by six o'clock.

This time, Dr. Cebulski talked to Quinn on his own for the first half of the appointment. Rob and I read *Psychology Today* magazines in the waiting room while a warm yellow light seeped out beneath the doctor's office door. I kept wondering what was happening on the other side of that door. On the drive to Ottawa, Quinn had been especially agitated, mumbling and erasing, rolling down the window to murmur into the wind. Medical appointments were clearly anxiety-inducing for him. I hadn't seen Quinn this wracked with OCD in days. *Damn*, I thought, as we drove down Highway 5. *There's no way he'll make it out for Halloween.*

Finally, the appointment was over and the door opened. Dr. Cebulski stood smiling at us. "You can come in now." When we walked into the office, which still felt like a living room, Quinn was at the coffee table leaning over a checkerboard. He looked up at us and grinned. "I beat him!" said Quinn.

"He's not a bad checkers player," said Dr. Cebulski.

Unlike the last time, the mood was light and jovial. It was obvious the doctor had broken through and got Quinn talking. Playing checkers was a brilliant technique. "He's coming along," said Dr. Cebulski. "Aren't you, Quinn?"

"Yep," said Quinn, who was attempting to leave the office without using his feet. This involved a kind of knee-walking.

"Hey, I've never seen that one before," I said.

Quinn was giggling. "Yeah, I kind of just invented this one."

Dr. Cebulski shook his head in amusement. "I have a challenge for you. Why don't you try putting one foot on the carpet before you leave. Just for a second."

Quinn knee-walked out of the office, stood up in the waiting room, then turned around to place the very top millimetre of his running shoe on the office carpet. He'd met the challenge, even if it was for a millisecond. He was giggling the whole time. At least he was happy.

Dr. Cebulski turned to Rob and me, smiling. "I can see you've been working hard on the exposure exercises. Whatever you're doing, it's working. Keep it up, all of you."

On the drive home Quinn didn't talk except to lament the pouring rain. "Rain Halloween bad. Bad Halloween rain."

Despite what the doctor had said about his progress, I wondered just how bad things might get that night.

An hour later I looked up to see my son wearing a black ninja costume and a black mask, wielding a cardboard sword in one hand and a bag for candy in the other. No clenched fists. Fists clenched no. I felt like doing cartwheels.

"Bye, Mummy!" He rushed outside into the rain to find the kids on the road. They always met at six at the bottom of our laneway on Halloween. They'd been doing it for years. They'd dash up and down our little road collecting chocolate bars as one shrieking neon-orange, ghost-sheeted ecstatic unit.

Half an hour later he arrived home, drenched, cheeks rosy, smiling. "Can you drive me down to Burnside Drive? It's raining too hard for me to walk all the way." Burnside Drive was a street full of century-old houses off Wakefield's main road. Burnside was where all the candy was. On Halloween, all the kids in Wakefield went to Burnside.

"Sure, get in the car. Let me grab my keys." *Could this really be happening?* I almost skipped to the car in the rain.

Just as we reached the main road, called River Road since it follows the river, Quinn called out, "Stop! I see my friends! They're at that house! Stop the car!"

I pulled over and we squinted through the rain-splattered car windows to see a cluster of costumed kids crowded on someone's front porch. "Wait, sweetie, before you get out, we need a plan. How about I meet you in half an hour or so at the ice-cream shop? They give out free ice cream. I'm sure your friends will be going there."

"Sure! See ya!" He slammed the door and ran off to meet his friends. I could hear them calling his name as he got closer. "Is that you, Quinn? Are you a ninja?" Quinn hadn't seen his school friends since the day he'd played soccer at recess and he hadn't been at school since the day of the cross-country race. I was delighted his friends actually remembered him.

I drove farther down the road. Everything was veiled in mist from the rain, draped in soft black velvet. Kids dressed as scarecrows and Draculas, as genies and Lego people danced along the sidewalk in their breathless pursuit of candy. I drove to an empty parking lot, hoping Quinn wouldn't notice me when he and his friends rushed by. I was killing time before meeting him at the ice-cream place, but still, I felt like a stalker of my own child. I was curious about how he'd be making out. Beside me, a maple tree was fully naked, its leaves a soggy orange dress circling its feet. When Quinn and his friends finally scurried by my car, I heard one of the boys say, "That's Quinn's mom in there," and they all looked my way. I felt like slinking down and hiding but it was too late.

Inside the ice-cream shop, a tiny clapboard house, I sat and talked with other parents about the rain. Finally, the boisterous group of boys arrived. I winked at Quinn and he smiled back. When he ordered his ice cream I overheard the serving girl asking him to speak up. Before they bustled out again, we made a plan to meet next at a house of friends of ours on Burnside.

Before I'd left home, I'd asked Rob what he suggested I do while Quinn was trick-or-treating. I couldn't exactly follow along behind him like a helicopter parent. He was way too old for that, even if he did have OCD. "Go to the Rooneys' house," said Rob. The Rooneys were friends of ours who lived near Burnside. They were documentary filmmakers who'd also started Theatre Wakefield and ran a summer film camp for kids.

"The Rooneys' house? Why?"

"Just do it. You'll see why."

Splashing through puddles as I traipsed my way in the rain to the Rooneys' house — their street was blocked off from traffic that night — I passed more hoards of trick-or-treaters: a self-assured get-out-of-my-way Hermione Granger leading a pack of witchy girls with less intimidating gaits, a boy (or possibly a girl) dressed as a barbeque, and someone who looked like a badass Shirley Temple. Little boys with husky voices always crack me up and here was one coming at me dressed as an old man stumbling and grouching along the street with a cane. I thought for a moment he was the real thing, an old geezer four-and-a-half-feet tall, out trolling the neighbourhood for free candy, but then he called me by name and I recognized his voice as belonging to a kid in our neighbourhood.

When I knocked on the front door of the Rooneys' house, Brenda Rooney answered. She's a striking woman in her sixties with straight, glossy silver hair and intelligent green eyes. As soon as she saw me, she took my wrist and pulled me inside. A lively Halloween party was happening and the house was filled with people I knew from Theatre Wakefield. Once in her living room she took me by both shoulders. "Laurie, my dear, I saw that email you wrote. Come with me." Leading me by the arm she escorted me into her kitchen, then sat me down at her kitchen table. "Wait here a second." She patted my back and left. A guy I knew was seated across from me, dressed as a garden gnome. Someone else at the table was dressed as a fallen fairy. This was the first year I hadn't even thought about a costume. The year before I'd been Carol Burnett. Brenda returned with a glass of red wine. She set the glass down in front of me. "Drink this, you need it. On second thought, take the bottle." She thunked the entire bottle of wine in front of me. I knew I wouldn't be able to stomach more than one glass that evening but adored the gesture.

I felt like something inside me was shaking loose, some unnamed raw emotion. I loved these people. They had no idea how much I needed all of this right now. *Wakefield is such a caring community! Thank God I sent that letter!* I took a gulp of wine. A friend named Zoe came over to say she wanted to treat me to a pedicure at the local spa because it was obvious I needed a break. People started telling me how sorry they were to hear about Quinn. Quinn had helped out as a stagehand in a play that Rob and I had been in the year before. They all knew Quinn. "He's such a nice kid," they said. "This is so sad. How can we help? Anything, anything at all."

"By doing exactly what you're doing." I took another swig of wine. "This is it right here. Just … talking to me. Thank you!"

Over an hour later, someone came to tell me that Quinn had just been at the door with his friends and had given the message to meet him later at the Wakefield General Store. The kids wanted to keep trick-or-treating, to go to their English teacher's condo because her boyfriend worked at Costco and the couple had lots of candy.

I set my wine down on the table. Had someone else embellished this message? How could all those words have come out of Quinn's mouth? Did one of his friends explain the long and detailed story?

At the Wakefield General Store parking lot I sat in the car watching rain pelt the windshield. Through the mist, the silhouettes of stick-bare trees wavered in the wind beside the river. Nobody else was around. I couldn't believe how long they'd been out there getting candy in this weather. Finally, Quinn in his ninja costume came sprinting toward the parking lot. He flashed me a wide grin and clambered into the back seat, ushering in a spray of rain along with him. Before I even got a word out, he said, "Whoa! You would not believe how many Kit Kats I think I have in here! And Coffee Crisps!

And yippee, Tootsie Rolls! And Peanut Butter Cups! Hey, there's some weird religious comic book in here, too. Oh, and bubble gum!"

I held my heart in my throat for more, dangling suspended in starlit space. And then more came, the sound of riffling through the candy bag, the crinkling of wrappers. "And Smarties! And Caramilk! There must be twenty of those in here! And Rolos! I love Rolos! Wow, and SweetTarts! And a toothbrush?"

Who was this child in my car?

I turned on the ignition, creeping at a snail's pace out of the parking lot, not wanting to drive too fast for fear of breaking the spell — whatever the spell was. I just knew I wanted this fragile moment never to end. I wanted this child in my back seat who was acting like the old Quinn to continue acting like the old Quinn.

We kept driving toward home, the dark trees shimmering and dancing in the rain, a bright flicker of moon rising up through my chest. Quinn was talking with a jubilance that I'd almost forgotten used to inhabit his every breath. "I had so much fun, Mummy! We went to every house on Burnside! I saw lots of funny costumes. Lots of kids I know. All my friends were there. Oh, and I want to go back to school."

I cranked up the windshield wipers to the fastest setting, not sure why my vision was suddenly so blurry. "Great idea! Yes, I think you definitely should!"

Quinn, are you really back? Did you fly through God's body and come out saying trick-or-treat on someone's doorstep? Have the child-stealing fairies brought you back to me? What is happening?

I didn't dare ask him what was happening. I didn't want to jinx it. All I knew was I felt like we were inside some kind of quietly enchanted miracle as I drove us home in the rain that night.

I seemed to have my son back.

CHAPTER 26

Every step in the dark turns out, in the end, to have been on course after all.

— John Tarrant, *Bring Me the Rhinoceros and Other Zen Koans that Will Save Your Life*

When we arrived at home, Quinn emptied the contents of his candy bag onto the living room floor and began sorting through chocolate bars, nacho chips, and various junky jellied things, talking non-stop about what candy looked interesting and what he'd throw away. There was no backtracking, no clenched fists, no erasing in our living room. Instead there was a regular happy kid with too much Halloween candy. The three of us lay sprawled on the floor around the mountain of junk food.

"Daddy, one kid went as a soccer player. I might do that next year. Or maybe I'll be Tom Branson from *Downton Abbey*. Oh, and you should have seen this one house. They gave out two chocolate bars each! I think some kids went back there twice. And you know Devon? Devon kept tripping because he had these dark glasses over his mask. We had to lead him around. And my English teacher? Her husband gave us so much candy from his work! Like, so much. Wanna see it?"

Quinn's voice had somehow become unleashed, was running free like a wild dog. I looked at Rob over a stash of potato chip bags in the throwaway pile. He gave me a look back that said, Is this real? Is this Quinn? Inside I was quietly exploding with joy.

Quinn went back to school immediately after Halloween. What felt so strange about his return to himself was the un-strangeness of it all, that Quinn acted as if he'd never been gone in the first place. He was so completely the old Quinn that I was often overcome with an eerie sense that the previous months had been a hideous dream, one of those dreams where you are so deeply lost and absent from yourself that you feel like you've been buried in the ground for centuries and have to claw your way out of it. But then you wake up and the bad dream is suddenly, miraculously ... over. Every day I'd say to Rob, "Is this really happening? He's back? He's actually outside with Liam and they're on their bikes? He's at the soccer field? He's down the street with the whole gang playing kick the can?"

One evening soon after Halloween, when I was still on shaky ground, still not convinced the OCD bully wouldn't make a return call, I attended another meeting of the Ottawa OCD Parent Support Group in the diner on the outskirts of Ottawa. Around the circle we shared our stories. One woman told us about her ten-year-old son who had an irrational fear of contamination from bats. "He stays locked in his bedroom most of the day just in case there might be bat colony lurking around. It's not as if we have any pet bats flying through the house. All I'm allowed to do is open his bedroom door a crack, just enough to hand him a Lysol wipe. He's missing his childhood because of this." An older couple told us about their twenty-something son who should, they kept saying, be living on his own now, not in their basement sleeping all day. "He sleeps all day because he stays awake all night putting our house in order. All the Coke cans have to be lined up perfectly on the shelves, all the soup cans have to be lined up according to his rules. The worst is the recycling. He monitors it. He goes through every square inch of lousy paper to make sure it really is recyclable. We're scared to throw stuff in there in case we've got it wrong. We go to bed early so he can get at it, start the ordering. It's driving us completely bonkers." This couple had never been to one of these meetings before and didn't yet know about exposure response prevention. The wonderful woman who runs the support group suggested they not enable the OCD because that only feeds it and makes it worse. She suggested they stay up late to upset his routine, throw the recycling out any way they felt like it. "Stop letting OCD boss you around," she told them.

One man, a lawyer with spiky silver hair, regaled us with stories about his twenty-year-old son who'd had OCD for twelve years but was now over it. "When Jake was about ten he decided to stop putting his feet on the floor. That made walking kinda hard. One night there were all these firemen in our building because of some emergency. They saw Jake trying to crawl on his hands and knees down the hallway and felt so bad for him that you know what they did? They came back the next week with a goddamned fancy wheel chair with a big red bow on it!" He slapped his knee and cackled. "They thought he was too poor to afford a wheelchair." After we all chuckled about this story the lawyer continued. "We finally got so fed up when he was nineteen that we sent him to an OCD treatment centre in Toronto. He was really excited about going but when we finally got there, he refused to get out of the car. My wife and I looked at each other in the front seat. We knew we had no choice but to tell him to get out. It's the saddest thing to have to boot your unwell kid out onto the street. But you know what? He got better. Not at the treatment centre. He never went inside. But when he found himself suddenly out on the street he had no choice but to pick himself up and figure it out. Somehow he did that. He figured it out. He found people's couches to sleep on. He found food. I don't know how he did it, but he came back home his old self again."

I nodded, trying to blink back the tears stinging my eyes. "Something like that just happened with us," I said. "At Halloween."

As one day passed into the next without a single sign of the OCD bully — our bright, funny boy completely himself again — I started to breathe normally, to sleep full nights. After a while, I realized I didn't have to tiptoe around the subject so lightly. Quinn and I were riding our bikes across the covered bridge one afternoon in late November, the wind whipping up from the river below and smacking our chilled hands. "So, Quinn, how did your OCD just go away like that on Halloween? It just disappeared. I'm still in awe. In one moment it was just, poof! Gone! How?"

Quinn was riding beside me, his hair blown back from the breeze inside the bridge. "Mummy, it didn't just go away in one moment. I had OCD all that night. I just wanted to be with my friends and to get candy more. The OCD kept wanting me to walk backward and count all my steps. I just pushed through. I just wanted to go out for Halloween."

And that was how he did it. With the determination of a soldier forging a raging river he made his way up that street crowded with costumed kids, broke through his thought-storms, and set himself free. Somehow on that Halloween night, not in a heartbeat or the pinprick of an instant after all, but gradually, door to door, he clawed his way back to himself.

The way I think of it now is a perfect storm of events leading up to Halloween. He'd built a cocoon around himself with his OCD so nothing could hurt him again after his grandpa's death. But everything began to change the day he climbed the tree, sending "Somewhere Over the Rainbow" into the sky to join my dad, finally saying goodbye to his grandpa for good. (I would read later that we humans have an association of goodness with aboveness, our upper field of vision associated with abstract thinking, religious thought, and hallucinations. The afterlife of many religions and much ancient mythology is associated with the sky — heaven, sky burials, Mount Olympus. Jim Davies writes about how the association of "up" with goodness has persisted across cultures and time even for the nonreligious. To this day I'm fascinated that Quinn chose to let my dad go while he was high up in a tree. Also, just the fact that he was in a tree at all for that moment of letting go meant a lot. I believe we're all deeply connected to trees more than we know — our ancient ancestors lived in them after all — and our collective psyche is still entwined in them. Kids the world over seem to feel this naturally every time they climb one.)

After that emotional healing, Quinn still needed to get rid of the OCD etched in the pathways of his brain. The habits had become too strong just to disappear on their own. That's where all the cognitive behaviour therapy came in. The ERP exercises that he and Rob had been working on so tirelessly did wonders. We were incredibly lucky that his brain was still young enough, still malleable enough, to change back so easily. Thank God for brain research. Then there was the letter. I never could have anticipated how much power there was in releasing our story out to our community like that. We needed normalcy back and we got it. But more than that, our desperate reaching out resulted in so much love and concern coming back to us that I believe some sublime community healing power was at work. I will be forever grateful for all the tender, passionate wide-open hearts of Wakefield, all tramping toward the sun's evening reflection on the river and toward easing other people's sorrows with a raised glass and a fundraiser.

And finally, there was Halloween. Some have suggested it was the costume. He wasn't Quinn that night, he was a powerful, masked, sword-spinning ninja. Others have suggested it was the magic of the night itself, when the veil between the worlds of the living and dead is at its thinnest, that perhaps my dad reached a hand down to Quinn that night and pushed him on his way. Gave a final nudge goodbye. Rob thought it was because the rewards of Halloween were so immediate and enormous (friends, free candy), unlike anything before where the rewards of "not doing OCD" were vague and long-term.

If I could see into the secret life of the world, I'd go with what Quinn said. His OCD vanished because he simply, finally, told it where to go.

JOURNAL

I'm walking down the hill of our white, slick road under the stars, snow creaking beneath my feet, the air like brittle glass. It's minus 33 degrees Celsius. Apparently this is the coldest winter on record.

Quinn gave his French speech to his class today. The topic was his love of cars. He said all the kids laughed and seemed to like his speech, especially the part where he told them he knew every single car in Wakefield, knew what kind of car each of their parents had, and even named several of those cars. "For instance, Tobias, your parents have a Kia Soul, and Jack, your dad drives a Ford Escape, and Luke, I noticed your parents traded in their Audi Allroad for a Mazda 3. Interesting choice." At the end of the speech he suggested his French teacher upgrade to a Ferrari. She told him she would if she could afford it.

Every day I am thankful for our unbelievable fortune in having Quinn back. Sometimes I just stand there gawking at him as he tells me some story about skiing after school with his friends, or as he demonstrates a new soccer deke in our living room, or when he sneaks into the cupboard for cookies and I catch him and he says, "Oh, jolly good, just perusing the shelves is all," in an English accent. I think: hold on to this moment. It's a gift as precious as life itself.

We escaped what could have been. Looking back now I see we took a trip around the dark side of the moon, not realizing it was a round trip. Rob kept saying that hope was all we had, that without it we were lost. I don't know how he knew this and I'm not sure he knows himself, but I am so grateful and awestruck that he did know. For myself, on some of those bleak days, hope was a no-show. I was once lucky enough to meet the author Barbara Kingsolver at a writers' festival in San Miguel de Allende and I remember her talking about hope. She said that hope isn't a state of mind, but something we actually do with our hearts and our hands, that helps us to navigate ourselves through difficult passages in life.

Sometimes the past hurls itself at me out of the blue. What happened to the three of us will live on in each of us in its own way. I can still call it up now, the magnitude of those days, the inconceivability of them, the sudden miraculous ending, and the weight of the relief of that ending. Often, Rob and I shake our heads and say, Can you believe that life threw us that curveball? That we almost lost the Quinn we knew but now he's off running around with his friends as if the whole thing never happened?

Does the ghost of the OCD monster still haunt us? Does it lie in wait in the dark corners of the house? Sometimes I imagine I see it shimmering in my periphery but more often I see it in my dreams, skulking back to steal my son again and ransack our lives. But as the months go by I believe more and more that it has been cast out of our family once and for all, banished to the badlands, a dictator deposed. Our family doctor mentioned to me recently that she believes that since Quinn did ERP so early on he's inoculated against OCD for good. I breathe in the hope that that's true and that the three of us are free to resume our regular lives like we didn't pass through purgatory at all.

Purgatory. I recall something I once heard about purgatory, that it's the stretch of time before death when you regret all the chances you missed to be human. Perhaps that's one positive thing that came out of this. When life as you know it is cycloned away from you, you learn something about yourself that you never would have had the chance to learn otherwise. I learned I'm lousy at emotional calamity. I can barely keep it together without falling to fractured pieces in a parked car. But I also learned something that all parents I'm sure must share but don't usually have the occasion to experience: that love for your children is so deep and bottomless that you are willing to throw everything away in a heartbeat if it means getting your child back. Not material things, that's easy, but everything else, too. I'd have gladly been stricken with OCD myself if it meant Quinn could be free of it.

As I walk through this ridiculously frigid night, I realize I've never been happier or more full of hope, as if the anguish of those days cleaved so deeply into my being that it made more room for joy. Just today I had an idea that I'd like to start a blog called "Fun Ways to Beat Back the OCD Monster" and I'd write about all that stuff Rob tried on Quinn. Maybe it could help other parents.

As for Quinn, I look to the poet and author Ann Michaels for wisdom. She wrote about how it's not a person's depth you must discover but their ascent. You look for their path from depth to ascent. I believe it's possible that this journey of Quinn's was something akin to a dark night of the soul, where, unlike most of us, he fully experienced death for what it is and when it was over, he came out stronger on the other side, with an understanding that perhaps many of us will never have.

An eleven-year-old auburn-haired boy gazes out at the wide expanse of the Gatineau River. He's standing on the rocky ledge of an island that he and his parents call Giant Caterpillar. It's the tail end of the summer holidays and the boy played offence on a soccer team, spent an exhilarating week at mountain-bike day camp, another week at soccer day camp, and a week at film camp where he and his friends wrote a script for a movie, then acted in it and helped film it. He also spent several long lazy weeks playing with his friends outside, riding his bike, swimming, and having sleepovers. He can't wait for grade six to start in a few days so he can see his school friends again. Looking out at the glass-blue expanse of the river that looks like a lake, he takes a handful of ashes from his mother and tosses them into the air over the water. His mother assumes he's going to shout something like, "Bye, Grandpa!" Instead, he throws the ashes and shouts, "Fuck off!" before giggling and taking a running leap off the ledge to do a cannonball into the water. The boy's exuberant face pops out of the water. "Now you try," he says to his mother. "Just don't do that cave woman jump."

FINAL WORD

Not long after Halloween we finally did get that sought-after appointment with the OCD cognitive behaviour specialist in Quebec. "He's fine now," I recall saying elatedly, after summing up our story. "He seems to have completely come out of OCD."

The doctor smiled but looked unimpressed. "That happens," she said. "OCD waxes and wanes." I sank down in my chair, feeling like a balloon that had just been pricked. "But sometimes," she added, "kids really do just get over OCD forever. With cognitive behaviour therapy they've learned how to beat it back before it even has a chance to start up again. They have the skills now. We don't know exactly why it totally disappears with some people and not with others. But it happens. We've seen it disappear entirely. Especially with kids. It could happen to Quinn."

Over a year later, this does seem to be what happened to Quinn. He is still free of OCD. Of course, it's possible it might return one day. But now he knows what to do. To his annoyance I occasionally ask him what he'd do if it returned. He shrugs and says, "I would just fight it back. I remember how."

And then he gets back to his lively eleven-year-old boy's life.

ACKNOWLEDGEMENTS

Thank you to the wonderful friends who read an early version of this book, or parts of it, and offered suggestions or encouragement: Tina Trineer, Kevin Shortt, Ilse Turnsen, Alison Gresik, Stephan Johnson, Brenda Rooney, Dawn Matheson, and Alison Wearing. I gratefully acknowledge the Canada Council for the Arts and the Quebec Arts Council for their generous grants. Thank you to my agent, Martha Webb, and all those at Dundurn Press. Thank you to the people of Wakefield, Quebec, for their wide-open hearts. You have no idea how far small gestures of kindness can go in changing one's world. Finally, I thank Tina Trineer, Christine Redl and Liam, Anna Lepine, and my mother, Tena Gough, for being there when we needed it most. (Mum, I know you don't like memoirs but I'm thanking you anyway!)

ABOUT THE AUTHOR

 Laurie Gough is the author of *Kiss the Sunset Pig: An American Road Trip with Exotic Detours* and *Kite Strings of the Southern Cross: A Woman's Travel Odyssey*, which was shortlisted for the Thomas Cook Travel Book Award and was the silver medal winner of *ForeWord Magazine's* Travel Book of the Year. Over twenty of her stories have been anthologized in literary travel books. She has been a regular contributor to the *Globe and Mail*, and has written for the *L.A. Times*, *USA Today*, *salon.com*, the *Toronto Star*, *Canadian Geographic*, the *Daily Express*, and *Caribbean Travel & Life*, among others.

Prior to her writing career, Gough left home at seventeen to live in Boulder, Colorado, received her B.A. in international development and English literature from the University of Guelph, and later completed a bachelor of education specializing in native education. She spent much of her twenties and early thirties hitchhiking alone around several continents, living in caves and hollowed-out redwood trees, and teaching school in Canada's sub-Arctic, Fiji, Malaysia, and Guelph, Ontario. She now lives in Wakefield, Quebec, with her family, who still often travel. Gough continues to write and teach memoir and travel writing courses.

www.lauriegough.com; www.travelwritinglife.com